ANGRY QUEER SOMALI BOY

A COMPLICATED MEMOIR

MOHAMED ABDULKARIM ALI

Printed and bound in Canada at Friesens. The text of this book is printed on 100% post-consumer recycled paper with earth-friendly vegetable-based inks.

Cover and text design: Duncan Noel Campbell, University of Regina Press
Copy editor: Kendra Ward, Proofreader: Katie Doke Sawatzky

Library and Archives Canada Cataloguing in Publication

Title: Angry queer Somali boy : a complicated memoir / Mohamed Abdulkarim Ali.

Names: Ali, Mohamed Abdulkarim, 1985- author.

Series: Regina collection.

Description: Series statement: The Regina collection

Identifiers: Canadiana (print) 20190113715 | Canadiana (ebook) 20190113863 | ISBN 9780889776593 (hardcover) | ISBN 9780889776609 (PDF) | ISBN 9780889776616 (HTML)

Subjects: LCSH: Ali, Mohamed Abdulkarim, 1985- | LCSH: Somalis—Canada—Biography. | LCSH: Muslim gays—Canada—Biography. | LCSH: Somalis—Canada—Social conditions. | LCSH: Somalis—Netherlands— Social conditions. | LCSH: Gay immigrants—Canada—Biography. | LCSH: Gay immigrants—Canada—Social conditions. | LCSH: Muslim gays—Canada—Social conditions. | LCSH: Muslim gays—Netherlands—Social conditions.

Classification: LCC HHQ75.8.A45 A3 2019 | DDC 306.76/6092—dc23

University of Regina Press
Saskatchewan, Canada, S4S 0A2
tel: (306) 585-4758 fax: (306) 585-4699
web: www.uofrpress.ca

10 9 8 7 6 5 4 3 2 1

We acknowledge the support of the Canada Council for the Arts for our publishing program. We acknowledge the financial support of the Government of Canada. / Nous reconnaissons l'appui financier du gouvernement du Canada. This publication was made possible with support from Creative Saskatchewan's Book Publishing Production Grant Program.

*This work is dedicated to
the one who gave me life.*

CONTENTS

XAMAR JAJAB, OR
BROKEN HAMAR

My grandparents were committed, well-indoctrinated communists, part of a wave of politicized African youth who emerged in the early postcolonial days following World War II. Some were trained in the finest universities of Russia, Yugoslavia, and China. All were eager to advance the ideological struggle of the hammer and sickle against the capitalist, imperialist West, which, to be fair, had raped the African continent over the preceding few centuries.

Still, socialism may have been a hard sell to nomadic Somali herders leading a subsistence life or to people struggling to stay alive on the streets of cities like Mogadishu. But my grandmother and grandfather were faithful to the teachings of Karl Marx. So faithful, that when my father inconveniently appeared in 1953, they quickly ditched him at my great-grandmother's house while they took off to pursue the class struggle somewhere in the desert.

Who could blame my grandparents though? Excitement was in the air as colonial empires collapsed. Following a military coup, Somalia finally adopted socialism as its political system in 1969. A Soviet-trained officer named Siad Barre ruled with an iron fist. Scientific socialism replaced Islamic custom and colonial laws.

By the time my father was a teenager, his grandmother, his only source of love and comfort, perished. She was his everything. She played father, mother, confidante, instructor and disciplinarian. All those functions went home to Allah with her. His whole world was draped in grief. Somalia entered unchartered waters as the 1970s dawned and my father's parents reappeared.

Since they had been early adopters of socialism, my grandparents were granted favours by Brother Siad, our supreme leader. My grandmother became the principal of a prestigious secondary school, in Mogadishu, or Hamar as locals called it. Her own son—my father—could've used a seat at this school, but grandma insisted he was not up to snuff. Her rejection of him was total.

★ ★ ★

This woman spent her youthful vigour, and his childhood, teaching nomads and their children about the modern world while he ached in vain for her affection and love. When given the chance to rectify the past, my grandmother continued to reject her son. She stayed strong in her wrong.

When my father grew into manhood, it was clear he wasn't cut out for a life of selfless brotherhood. He turned away from the country's utopian ideals and became a firefighter in the United Arab Emirates. He left Somalia to make his fortune and settled in an industrial town named Ruwais. He began working for the national gas company. Skyrocketing oil prices filled the coffers of the Persian Gulf kingdoms and they imported millions of labourers from the newly independent states in Africa and Asia. He chose capitalism and conspicuous consumption. I saw him as a philistine, but he was in tune with the flow of history, unlike his parents. Socialism, despite its lofty promises, brought little material comfort to Somalis.

Meanwhile, Brother Siad was betrayed by the Soviets when they shifted their patronage to

Ethiopia, Somalia's ancient nemesis. In 1977, after a disastrous war over the Ogaden, Ethiopia's Somali region, Brother Siad and his henchmen panicked and turned on their own people. As the French journalist Jacques Mallet du Pan observed in 1789, *the Revolution, like Saturn, starts to consume its own children.*

And so it was in Somalia nearly two hundred years later.

When my father was a youth, Somalis married young and Somali women had children early. Children were left in the care of their mothers, grandmothers, and aunts while the young women pursued the pleasures of life with their husbands.

Youthful marriages were common for various reasons, the foremost being life expectancy. Recent Somali history had been dominated by internal strife, foreign domination, and wars with its neighbours. The first ones to die were young men, so before they met their end on the battlefield, their bloodline's continuation had to be ensured. In our culture, children were raised in the mother's family but identified with the father's clan. If a woman was left widowed, the extended family jumped into action, relieving the mother of some of the burdens.

This custom received an update when our beautiful land achieved freedom. Those sent abroad for study or work were married off before leaving. For example, my father's first marriage, to my biological mother, was to ensure his continued, periodic return from Ruwais to Mogadishu. Clan tensions were always high, and marriage assuaged that pressure. A young woman went from her paternal home to her in-laws and had little room to consider her own personhood.

Before independence, Somali women were not autonomous. Despite the horrors it wrought, the regime of Brother Siad took quite a progressive stance on women's rights. Women were encouraged to attend school, to avoid circumcising their daughters, and to organize themselves through the Somali Women's Democratic Organization. Divorce was made easier with the introduction of the Family Law, taking power away from the mosque, the traditional domain for settling domestic disputes.

I was born October 20, 1985.

My mother was the most delightful creature to me, or that is how I reconstruct her from memory. I called her *hoyo*, or mother, but her name was Dahaba, which means gold in Arabic. She was my father's first cousin and their union had been arranged by their families.

I can't say I remember any of his visits during my early childhood. Turmoil was in the air, as the space

I was born into soon became levelled by ancient rivalries and bloodlust.

On the eve of New Year's 1990, a strange man appeared at the gate of my mother's home. Everyone embraced him as I hid behind my mother's legs.

Go on, give your father a kiss.

His bushy moustache scratched my face and I recoiled in horror. I cried and they laughed. I can still picture their amused faces. There was a certain tragedy to the whole affair. The sight of the green gates of the house, the sandy courtyard, the vanishing faces of my family, and the noisy refrigerator that held my bottle of Fanta became a mirage. I returned to them often but were my memories an accurate reflection of the experience? Did nostalgia cover the painful parts with dust? I peered down at the iron grate covering the fire pit. I stopped crying and my mother took me inside to bathe. It was my final dip in the oasis before the whole country was swept up in the violence of clan warfare ... and my body and soul started to float from the Indian Ocean to the Persian Gulf.

★ ★ ★

As the rebels closed in on Mogadishu and looted military facilities along the way, we waited for our flight to Abu Dhabi. My father insisted I eat, but the best I could do was move the soggy veggies around my plate. Before departing my mother's home, I posed for pictures in a pressed outfit. Years later, I received a call from my mother and she mentioned these photos.

I wish you had smiled, even just a little.

We drove down a long and winding road to Ruwais. To our right was the expansive palace of the emir. His photos lined the highway; in some, he received flowers from children. It was funny that despite their hatred for the Soviet Union, Arab tyrants copied, without attribution, Soviet propaganda.

You have two sisters and one brother. Your new mother is a lovely woman. You can call her hoyo. Don't worry, I won't tell your mom.

I stared at my father. The road seemed endless and the palace of the emir was still visible.

How many people lived in the palace? I saw pens holding camels and birds. There were no humans in sight.

As we turned into a cul-de-sac, I was overcome with anxiety. The landscape was more ordered than the desert surrounding the airport or the emir's palace. My new relations stood in the threshold of my new home. The two girls embraced me and helped me lug my suitcase inside. For the first time in my brief life I was silent. I went to my new room and threw my face into the pillow. I had no siblings before arriving at their home. I hadn't eaten anything since leaving my mother's house, and I cried thinking about the noisy refrigerator and the Fanta I had left behind.

The eldest girl I'll call Fadumo and the younger one Ebyan.

Fadumo was tall and awkward whereas Ebyan was short and fiery. Fadumo had on some contraption that stopped her from moving her mouth. Apparently, it was to correct the effects of lockjaw. Whenever her older sister displeased her, Ebyan shouted *Crooked Mouth!* at her. She deployed the epithet with such precision that I took note. Antagonism became the bedrock of their sisterly bond. Upon meeting them, I felt a sense of safety, as though these girls were going to look out for me.

The boy, corpulent and testy, I'll call Isaac. He was younger than me by three years. He was the boy whose parents were still together; he was our father's youngest and his mother's only son. I was in Ruwais as a guiding light to him.

I was robbed of my mother for Isaac's benefit. And even at my tender age, I knew if someone took something from me, they became my mortal enemy, blood be damned.

My new *hoyo* was Samira.

The fact that she and one of Saddam Hussein's wives shared the same name could be a coincidence.

Samira's youngest sister, Yasmin, lived with us as well. She was unpaid help—in other words, a slave.

We children spent our free time riding around the development on our bikes, until these were stolen by Kuwaiti refugees. Then they stoned the house and punctured the tires of my father's car. This was because my stepmother yelled *long live Saddam* when they rode around the neighbourhood to celebrate their country's liberation from the tyrant. Such fine people, these Kuwaitis!

Back in Hamar, there had been no boys in my vicinity. I had felt no need to defend what was mine since the adults around me had happily indulged me. In Ruwais, I was enrolled in a nearby school. Every morning, we gathered in the playground and sang the national anthem. There I encountered boys my own age. They were dressed in long white shirts akin to tunics, called *kandurah*. Since the words for *African* and *slave* are interchangeable in Arabic, my schoolmates thought hurting me was their holy right. I showed them what I was about and they didn't like it.

Samira, meanwhile, had carried the burden of being widowed at a very young age and she and her daughters didn't know how to cope. They had relocated to the Middle East when Samira married my father, her second husband.

Fadumo and Ebyan's father was rarely mentioned. Like my mother, their father was a mythical creature who'd been usurped. The silence and secrecy encouraged the myth making. From time to time, Samira shouted awful things about their father.

If he were alive, you wouldn't want to know him!

I gazed at the open wound in their spirit and found, in their longing for their father, kindred spirits.

My father didn't stay with us often. He lived in a compound built for gas-company workers. He spent two months on land, followed by a one-month break, and then two more months on a gas installation at sea. Even though he brought me to be near him, I rarely saw him.

Listen, I'll take the children to London. My sister will get us settled, my stepmother said one day to my father.

My father took this in.

London sounds like a dangerous place. I'm not sure if I want the boys growing up in that kind of environment.

My stepmother went back to flipping the pages of a catalogue.

Should we stay here? You told me the other day the government doesn't want us here. I'll be damned if they send me to a war zone. These Arabs are heartless. London, take it or leave it.

He knew he was cornered.

Promise me this: Mohamed must always speak to his mother. I made that promise to her and I have to keep it.

She kept flipping pages.

You heard me?

She looked up and rested the catalogue on her lap.

She can call him whenever she wants. I'm not the sort of person to stand between a mother and son.

TORN DESERT FLOWERS

Long before the rise of monotheism in Somalia, girls had been circumcised. In Somali culture, it is believed that the modification of a girl's genitalia curbs her sexual appetite. The clitoris is shaved off, the labia sewn shut, and a small triangular hole left at the bottom of the vagina. In Somalia, boys were not privy to the goings-on of a cutting.

The scene was surreal. It took place a few months after my arrival. Isaac and I were parked in front of the television and my father put on wrestling. I heard a knock on the door and rushed to answer. Before me stood a woman with scars on her face and my stepmother welcomed her in. Samira offered her some tea, which she declined. The women and my father disappeared down the hall, to the girls' bedroom. For the next few hours, I heard the screaming of two young girls. They cried while their mother, along with their new father, held them down as a stranger cut off parts of their bodies. Was this violence contagious? I felt weak for not rushing in to aid my new sisters. Instead, I watched hulking men throw each other around. I focused on their muscles instead of the bloodied water my father carried to and from the bathroom. They modified the girls in Ruwais because they knew it would be next to impossible to do it in Europe.

As the old order of socialism versus capitalism came to an uneventful end, we were swept westward like particles of Chernobyl fallout dust. My stepmother, the boy, the two girls, and I boarded a plane bound for London to meet her sister. I had no real mother to hug or father to admire. Instead, I was in the care of a mentally frail and culturally ancient woman.

THE DUTCH DISEASE

There's a saying in Dutch that translates to "God made the Earth but the Dutch created the Netherlands."

Pray for me as we glide through an African boy's journey through one of Europe's more narrow cultures. It begins this way.

My stepmother decided in the spur of the moment that she'd rather get off the plane with the kids at Schiphol, the main international airport of the Netherlands, instead of in London, our intended destination. She didn't inform her sister, patiently waiting for her in the United Kingdom, for about a week.

Dutch immigration officers must've been given a fright as this heavily pregnant Somali woman lurched toward them.

Her tale of woe lined up with Dutch asylum policy. The truth was, she knew nothing about the horrors she described in her testimony to the refugee board, as we had spent the previous few years luxuriating in a Middle Eastern exurb while bombs rained down on Somalia's northern cities.

In retrospect, this was a necessary lie.

Years later, as we exchanged the Netherlands for Canada, we made a pitstop to see my father in the Emirates. Seated a few rows behind us and screened off by the lovely KLM crew, was a screaming man being subdued by Dutch immigration officers. In her halting Dutch, Samira asked the flight attendant what the matter was. Apparently, he had been rejected for asylum and was being sent back to East Africa.

Had Samira told the truth in 1991, we too would've been cast back to the Horn.

Instead, we had been temporarily housed in an apartment in the city of Alphen aan den Rijn, and a short time later, or so it seemed to me, we were in a refugee camp in Gelderland.

Gelderland is in the west of the Netherlands and is considered part of the Dutch Bible Belt.

The camp was in a farmer's field. Each family was assigned a trailer. On television, I watched American boys with long hair singing about their fears and broken hearts. I felt guilty looking at their pale and sinewy bodies, often shirtless. Their lack of modesty and religious convention excited me.

It was in Gelderland that, once again, Arab hatred of blackness reared its ugly head. My stepmother was in line at the remittance office in the camp. She was still heavily pregnant and not paying attention. When it was her turn, the man behind her mumbled something in Arabic and pushed her. Samira, never the one to back down from a fight, steadied herself and socked him. Her ring lodged in his face and once out, his cheek split wide open and blood gushed everywhere.

It taught him never to fuck with a pregnant Somali woman again.

Shortly after our arrival, we welcomed my youngest sister. She was named Ismahan.

She was our bundle of Dutch joy. As we got ready to leave the camp, my stepmother was told by a social worker that she risked her application for asylum if she cut my sister.

Is it legal for boys to be circumcised?

The social worker felt less tense about this.

Natuurlijk!

Not only was it legal but the state footed the bill. Samira eyed me.

We left the camp in 1993 for a village named Schipluiden. It was within walking distance of Delft, the town renowned the world over for producing counterfeit china.

Newcomers were enrolled in courses that taught Dutch and explained the history and customs of our new home. Members of the community volunteered to show newcomers how to do the shopping, use the bank, and sign up children for school and recreation.

We were paired with a Moroccan family who lived down the street. The head of this family drove me to my procedure in Delft. On the way there, he said that after my circumcision, I would be a full member of the *umma*, or community of believers.

The Dutch disease claimed its pound of flesh from my dick.

I recovered in the attic. Dutch attics, or *zolders* as they are known locally, are narrow and ours had a tiny window instead of a skylight. These were the places Dutch bohemians used to live and Dutch art was dreamt up. I spent my time looking up at the ceiling and reading the newspaper to pass the time. When I finished reading, I ate bits of the paper.

There was no bathroom, so I pissed into a bucket. To satisfy my hunger on the weekends, when Samira slept in well past noon, I ate more newsprint than usual. My dick healed and the pinkness of the head frightened me.

I could no longer pull the skin back or run my fingers under it. In Somalia boys weren't circumcised at birth but cut later in childhood. I didn't know this at the time and my ignorance of this led me to believe that Samira wanted to inflict unnecessary harm on me.

Modifications in the name of Allah, our Lord, tied me to my stepsisters.

Ismahan was a ray of sunshine in those days of juvenile uncertainty. My stepmother bemoaned how being a Dutch child spoiled her.

She is my gift to Queen Beatrix.

Being born in the Netherlands didn't spoil her, but we did.

For example, we negotiated with her when she threw a fit.

In Somalia, she'd get slapped across the face and told to cut it out.

A favourite tactic of hers was to throw herself, head first, onto the floor. She did this most often in grocery stores when her mother refused her something.

I hope she didn't suffer long-term effects from her lovemaking to the floor.

We didn't know what to make of Schipluiden, despite living there for over a year. Samira didn't know how to pronounce it when relatives called. Tired of repeating herself, she told them we lived in Delft.

People got around by bicycle, but my stepmother didn't take to the Dutch mode of transport. Driving was out of the question since gas prices were too high. We were used to the subsidized gasoline prices that we had in the Middle East.

Sorghum porridge gave way to the Dutch porridge. After learning from her brother in Sweden that Europeans made their white bread with gelatin, an ingredient supposedly derived from pigs, Samira forbade us from eating it. My lunches were a mix of leftovers and whatever egg concoction she made that morning.

The spice and aroma puzzled my little white friends and they teased me about it. I begged her to make me cheese sandwiches with a schmear of butter. She wasn't going to buy it so she baked bread at home. From that point on, my lunches were Dutch. This was a victory in my quest to become a Nederlander.

One day, a knock came at the door. Before me was a squat, dark man with woolly hair. He had a suitcase and a smaller bag resting atop it.

There's some black guy here!

Samira made her way to the door.

That's not some guy, that's your father!

Why didn't I ever recognize him?

He was some stranger that I didn't yearn for or cry for at night.

My father didn't know how to be a parent.

What role models did he have?

His idea of parenting was to provide us with things. Whenever he called, he asked me what I wanted. He never asked how I was feeling or what I dreamt of.

Perhaps, I was asking for too much.

Without him, I could have been one of those kids in Somalia, in the back of pickup trucks, manning an anti-aircraft gun and smoking a contraband cigarette. He saved me from a life of war but didn't bother explaining it. I was left to realize it on my own. He assumed that I'd have no questions about my mother, or why I was living in this foreign place with his new wife and my new siblings.

My father stayed about a month. Nothing memorable happened.

★ ★ ★

One way we stayed in touch with my father was by sending messages on cassette tapes. The first recording was shortly after we moved to Schipluiden. My stomach was in knots because I didn't know what to say. The others recorded first. I thought I had escaped the whole thing by hiding in the bathroom. Between the bathroom door and the ceiling was a glass panel. I looked up to behold Samira's disapproving face.

Warya! She shouted the word for boy in Somali. *Warya! What are you doing!?*

I feigned shock.

I'm taking a shit, hoyo.

She got down from the chair and yelled at me through the door.

You better hurry up. We're done waiting for you.

I strained to form sentences in Somali. My tongue had shifted from Somali to Arabic to Dutch.

How many more tapes?

In the end, I was sending messages in English, rendering Dutch, Arabic, and Somali obsolete.

It was in Schipluiden that Samira began abusing me.

At dinner one night, I kept eyeing Isaac's plate while greedily scarfing down my meal. I asked for seconds. I kept my eyes glued to his plate. I was full but I kept my eyes on his plate. Instead of chastising me for my voracity, she put the pot of pasta in front of me.

If you're hungry, eat this.
I'm not hungry anymore.
Your eyes say otherwise.

She kept watch as I forced the noodles down. I tried my best not to cry.

Samira grew bored with life in Schipluiden.

Her only black friend was a woman from the Congo, then called Zaire. Samira didn't speak French, so they resorted to using their scant Dutch to talk. They usually sat in companionable silence.

There was nothing my stepmother hated more than the sound of French.

The wife of our Moroccan neighbour was dull and Samira avoided her. Even though they both spoke Arabic, Samira didn't see the point. Her wish was granted when in 1994 we moved from Schipluiden to a town southeast of Rotterdam with an even more unpronounceable name.

Papendrecht was a bedroom community near a city named Dordrecht. The residences in the complex were flat-roofed houses placed atop one another, with stairwells to access the upper residences. Openings on the sides of the square led either to a street or a parking lot. In the centre was a courtyard, with a giant tree holding on for dear life. This was where I grew into a lanky teenager with strange, and sometimes criminal, friends.

The first Somali family we met in Holland lived upstairs from us. The kids were not daring and this made them uncool. They were only interested in reading the Quran and following their parents' wishes. I wanted zero parts of what they had to offer.

Soon after we arrived, another Somali family moved to the neighbourhood. They were the family of the boy who became my best friend. His name was Yusuf, and his mother had lived through the bombing of northern Somalia. A piece of shrapnel was lodged in her eye, which earned her the nickname Iron Eyes.

Somalis are ferocious when it comes to nicknames. My family had nicknames for one another as well. Mine was Sri Lanka, on account of my hair and ambiguous appearance. My brother's was Tyson as he was prone to outbursts of violence, often directed at inanimate objects such as his glasses. Fadumo's was Giraffe and Ebyan's Lion, for her ferocity and flat nose. My stepmother's was Hippo and Ismahan was called Fiino Fiino, after a type of thin noodle Somalis enjoy.

Yusuf and his family were a mixed bag. Not everyone had the same father and some didn't even belong to his family. Two of Yusuf's brothers were actually his first cousins. Yusuf had a younger brother named Daud and an older sister. She, like our

Ebyan, was a hell-raiser and drove Iron Eyes into fits of rage followed by streams of tears.

Yusuf was a kleptomaniac. Samira didn't want him coming over and I made up excuses as to why.

Another thing you ought to know about him was that he was my first love. He was the first boy I felt such longing for. You mightn't think a nine-year-old capable of such feelings or of knowing the difference between love and lust, but I did. He showered me with kisses, although I pretended not to like it. When he greeted me with hugs, his scent invaded my nostrils and inflamed my loins. He, in his criminal glory, became the template for the sorts of men I sought out in adulthood.

In 1994 I enrolled at a school named Bovenkruier, which translates to "smock mill." Much like the rest of the neighbourhood, the school's name was a reference to the local windmills.

I was in the fourth-grade class of Ms. Wilhelmina, or *mejuffrouw* Wilhelmina, as the Dutch had it. She made sure everyone welcomed me. The class was largely made up of native Dutch children, with a splattering of Antillean, Surinamese, and Vietnamese. I was one of two Somali students. The Somali girl's last name sounded, to my southern Somali ear, like the word for rabbit.

Her older brother, who was in the same grade as Ebyan, was menacing and mocked my discoloured teeth. My teeth were the object of ridicule in that school for years. It was the first time my appearance was made fun of. I stopped smiling, and when I did, I made sure not to expose any teeth. Laughing with my mouth open was out of the question unless my hand covered it. Many of the things I grew to hate about myself took root during this time.

Anything I did in that family of mine got me into trouble.

Why are you always inside? Go outside and be like the rest of the boys!

Whenever Samira had visitors, I was called back in. I made tea and served sweets.

You are lucky to have a son like Mohamed.

I was at the mercy of people unmoored from their usual roles back home. My stepmother played both father and mother. When her madness put her out of commission, her daughters became deputy tyrants. I rued the day I disobeyed.

Our sudden appearance in this strange land left us vulnerable and isolated. By acting out in sadistic ways, we asserted ourselves. We had no aunts or uncles to relieve us from paternal suffocation. When relatives visited from abroad, I saw the same struggles playing out in their families. The despondency was legible in their spirits and in the dark jokes they told. Many of Samira's relations had done well under the socialist regime in Somalia. Now they were rootless beggars calling on the white folks they had denounced back home. The bitterness was strong and a sense of defeat crept into their lives. Their exile marked a return to Islam. The belief was that we had turned away from Allah and exile and beggary was our reward.

Ebyan hated my father as much as I hated her mother. I understood her loathing, but she didn't understand mine. According to her, I should be grateful her mother brought me to a peaceful country, made me food, and woke me for school every morning. She didn't think the violence against me was that bad and joined in. She delighted in humiliating me in front of others. Once, she slapped me across the face in front of some neighbourhood kids. They saw the anger in my eyes and told her to apologize. She refused.

The look in his eyes will kill you!

She told me to toughen up.

One way Ebyan advanced her program of abasement of me involved phone booths. She'd shove me into one and dial toll-free adult chatlines and then put me on. She told me what to say when the men on the other end asked me what I was wearing.

Their heavy breathing excited me. I didn't know why I felt this way. She told me to say I was a little girl. The men said they'd finger me until juice ran down my leg. One promised to force his dick in and impregnate me. Another would sodomize me with a vibrator until I bled.

The scariest call was when I accidentally told one of them where I was. He told me to hop on the bus to Rotterdam and meet him at the central station.

Looking back, it is clear she was trying to humiliate me. But I returned to the chat lines on my own. Those men, with their ejaculatory breathing, desired me. I felt precious when I got them off. I promised to call back. I was a star to these perverts. I enjoyed the control I had over their desires.

Please don't get me pregnant. My dad will beat me!

They promised to take care of me and the baby.

I wonder if Ebyan remembers any of this? I doubt she'd admit to it. I ought to be grateful, though, that she helped me unearth my libertine urges.

(S)HE DOES NOT KNOW HER BEAUTY

When she was a toddler, Ismahan was wracked by nightmares. She fell asleep on the couch or floor and stirred. It seemed like she was shaking her head. Her expression was pained and Samira said the devil was taunting her. Samira's solution was the Quran.

Read her a verse or two. Run your hands over her face. Make sure not to wake her. I don't need the crying right now.

I parked myself beside her and recited bits of Quran I knew. I spat, sans saliva, into my hands and like a healer, ran them over her fragile head. I wanted to do battle with Satan so my delight could sleep easier.

The feeling of helplessness was the only steady thing in my life. Being a victim of circumstance was the way I felt empowered. Fantasy is where I was at my most powerful. I spun tales of grandeur in my head. I dreamt of becoming a gold dealer in South Africa with a pet cheetah. Other times, I hobnobbed with the fashion elite as the designer for a legendary fashion house. I constructed characters and turned those I hated into monsters. I was strong because I withstood pain. Cunning because I lied without remorse. I rooted for the evildoers on TV because their traits were admirable. Self-sacrifice, in my mind, led to betrayal. Showing vulnerability made me a target for predators. I declined being good because there were no rewards. Wickedness was my intention.

One day as I played soccer with a bunch of neighbourhood kids, I leapt into the air to kick the ball. One of them referred to my move as a *ballerina kick* and called me *ballet girl*. The name stuck. My stepmother used it.

Mohamed, stop being such a ballet girl!

Even though our household was largely made up of women, femininity equalled weakness. My twists of the wrists made me less than a real boy.

Why do you act like a girl? Why can't you just be like your brother?

There was no question of Isaac being like me. Why did they want their brother or son to be like me? I was a ballet girl.

The violence at home always felt unexpected. I never knew what direction a slap or heart-stopping scream would come from. My stepmother delighted in wringing my ears until an intense heat emanated from the side of my head. I was told not to cry while being lashed with a belt or radio cord. I took slippers to the face. My body and mind began to drift apart. As my corporeal senses were inflamed with pain, my mind drifted into the next day.

Tomorrow, it won't hurt as much. Stay there.

I yearned for control. I wanted to impose myself on someone else. I retreated into my thoughts.

I began to envision scenes of great carnage. The blender exploding in my stepmother's face as she made traditional hot sauce. Shards of glass piercing her eyes and the heat inflaming her sockets. I prayed the bleaching creams gave her cancer. Her fat ass wasting away and me laughing as she struggled to swallow food. I'd deny her pain medication to extend her suffering. I dreamt of boiling water and pouring it on her face as she slept.

After one of my beatings, I had to wash my brother's pants, by hand. They were coated in mud. I took one of the legs and began stuffing it down my throat.

I kept going until I felt vomit coming up. I breathed through my nose as the bile burned the back of my throat. With a violent jerk of the pants, the vomit poured out. Euphoria!

My father thought that by taking me from Somalia he had shielded me from the spectre of violence and the ensuing cult of death. Sadly for him, I was tainted. I lived in my head all the time. My mind was a sanctuary from all the violence. In order to satisfy, my thoughts had to be more violent. Self-harm alone wasn't cutting it. I yearned for transgression.

The fantasies became more elaborate. I had to act out this rage. I began fighting boys and girls at school and in the neighbourhood. I couldn't contain it any longer. In the spring, I threw rocks at ducklings. I hit one in the neck but it didn't die right away. Instead, its neck dangled underwater while its body swam in circles. The helpless mother tried saving her spawn.

This behaviour was in sharp contrast to the diligence with which I treated my school work. I excelled at geography and stole an atlas from school. I studied the world map with glee. Rajasthan, Ulan Bator, the Amazon, Anhui, Conakry, the Zambezi, Kalamazoo, the Haud, and so on. These exotic places were an escape from my existence in the flattest place on Earth.

If I couldn't move, perhaps I ought to kill them all. I was diagnosed with psychopathy and the school recommended counselling. Samira balked at the idea and insisted the cure lay in my continued study of the Quran and praying five times a day. If Allah was something she held dear, I wanted none of it. At night, I gazed at the ceiling.

Even if You are there, I don't believe in You.

Once a week we attended Quranic classes, at the home of the Somali family upstairs. I spent countless hours listening to my stepmother as she recited ancient lines to us. Her corpulent body stretched out on the couch as we sat on the floor with the holy book on our laps. If a mistake was made, my reward was a tongue lashing or an object to the head.

When Saturday rolled around, we recited, from memory, everything we had learned the day before. The teacher never smiled. A job well done was met with a nod. It was our duty to learn the Quran, so why did we expect a reward?

Yusuf was like me when it came to our faith. We had no interest in being observant or being constrained by *halal* or *haram*, what is lawful and what is forbidden. We watched porn and listened to explicit music from America. We wanted zero parts of the culture we were born into. How were we going to be Somali outside of Somalia, the source of our

Somaliness, or Somaliniimo? Was identity tied to a piece of land or was it a state of mind? For us, these questions were too large. We wanted to show off our sneakers and smuggle fireworks from Belgium.

As soon as we got our travel documents, we went on vacation to Sweden. Samira's mother had been granted asylum there and lived in Gothenburg. This woman was my grandmother now, in lieu of the one I left behind in Somalia. We boarded a train in Dordrecht and made our way to Hamburg, where we changed trains. The urban form gave way to greenhouses, fields teeming with dairy cows and the occasional windmill. Gliding through Jutland, we crossed a bridge connecting Denmark and Sweden. Below us laid the wreckage of war and Viking loot. When it was time to eat, we marched into the dining car. Beside us was an older Dutch woman who told my stepmother never to travel further east than Berlin. It was odd to see the pair connect over their loathing of the Slav.

We took a taxi from the train station. Our driver was a Kurd from northern Iraq. As soon as Samira found this out, all conversation ceased. She was an admirer of Saddam Hussein.

I suppose monsters have a special affinity for each other. In Samira's mind, Saddam was the saviour of the oppressed Muslims in the Middle East.

He was the only one capable of destroying Israel and the Jews and bringing about a Palestinian state. His crimes against Muslims within Iraq and in Iran weren't considered.

Those people are heretics. They have images in their mosques!

We were dropped off at a beautiful housing complex, replete with Swedish girls swinging from the monkey bars. It had the utopian feel that my grandmother's generation strived for back in Somalia. If the buildings could speak, they'd shout, *From each according to his ability, to each according to his need!*

The apartment was cozy and grandma told us the Swedes came by every few years and applied a fresh coat of paint. She loved this land and spoke of how well they treated her.

I used to detest white people until I moved here!

She encouraged us to play with her little Swedish neighbours. I wasn't interested. Their language sounded like a stroke patient trying to whistle. Instead, I wandered a nearby park and had imaginary conversations in English.

My grandmother was unusually sweet for a Somali woman. This sweetness hid a life of travails. Despite cutting all her daughters, she was a modern and politically conscious woman. When socialism infected Somalia, she sent her children to be educated abroad, and some of her sons fought in the irredentist war against Ethiopia. Learning was very important to her because she never had the chance to go to school herself. Samira used to regale us with stories of her mother in Mogadishu.

Your grandmother used to snatch the hijab off my head. I wasn't married and men wouldn't talk to me if I went around covered up.

At fifteen, grandma's mother died suddenly and she was expected to care for her younger sisters. Her hard work put her younger sisters through school and both married well. Upon achieving success, they turned their backs on my grandmother. They had no time for her lack of refinement. The circles they travelled in were better-heeled than the semi-nomadic man my grandmother married. All three sisters lived in Scandinavia but never saw each other.

My grandmother's neighbour, whose children and grandchildren lived in Holland, had given her wooden clogs. The neighbour had bought them for her grandkids but they declined the gift. She wanted my grandmother to give them to us. They didn't fit anyone, except me. Since the clog fit, I had to forfeit my Somali origin.

Once we got back to Papendrecht, Samira said that Isaac and I needed some sports in our lives. I hated the idea.

Why do you hate things boys are supposed to love?

We joined a soccer club near the town centre, past the mall where Yusuf and I loitered and swiped cheap trinkets. The club was nestled between the stately homes of Papendrecht's great and good. Our team's sponsor was an emblem of Dutch industry, Fokker. The Fokker building was next to the club and the executives passed through, from time to time, to wish us well.

I made no effort to impress during tryouts so I was placed on the lowest team in my age bracket. All this running around seemed stupid to me. This wasn't going to expand my mind. The team was coached by the father of one of the players. I liked him until he criticized me while we were driving to a match.

Mohamed, you needn't be so fanatical with the ball. You can afford to pass the ball. Your job is to defend the goal, not score.

I nodded in agreement. The Dutchman was always right.

Not all ignorance was that subtle. My teammates sang songs about Ali Baba and called me Cacaface or Zulu Lips. They saw no conflict between emulating American rappers and degrading my blackness. This taunting came to a grinding halt when a Surinamese boy joined the team. He was one of two West Indian boys on the team. The other one wasn't black and felt more at home with the white supremacists in training. The team captain, our coach's son, initiated our new teammate. While in the shower, the captain tugged at the new boy's dreadlocks. Despite being asked to stop, he kept at it. Next thing I knew, the white kid was eating hands. The Surinamese kid grabbed him by the neck and smashed him into the wall. After that, none of their pale asses came for me or my brethren.

My father, during this period, was no hero. He visited a few times a year, but half the time he called on other people. We were an obligation instead of a blessing.

I joined him on one trip to his relatives' house near Rotterdam. Isaac didn't want to leave his cartoons so it was just me. We drove for a few hours and arrived in another nondescript housing project. His kin were waiting outside and after they performed the compulsory salutations, we went inside. I was told to go play with my cousin. This boy was a few years older and really fat. We went up to his room and my eyes landed on a red fire truck. I asked if I could play with it.

You can but only if you touch my pee-pee.

I went downstairs to rejoin my father. My cousin brought the truck downstairs and turned the sirens on, which annoyed his parents.

Warya! Why don't you and Mohamed go play outside.

I said I wanted to stay inside.

Don't disobey your elders.

My father shot me a stern glance. The boy asked for his father's car keys and we sat in the backseat. He undid his pants and pulled my hand onto his dick. I watched myself being grabbed. My body went limp and he handed me the truck.

See, that wasn't so bad.

As we got ready to leave, he wanted to hug me. I stepped back and ran into the car.

What did you think of your cousin?

I wish I had the guts to tell my father the truth, but knowing what kind of person he was, he wouldn't have believed me.

I remember when I lost all confidence in my father.

It began with an argument about whether his mother ought to come visit us. Having never met the woman, it was an exciting prospect for me. But Samira wasn't having it and called the old woman a whore.

He shot back by calling her a whore.

This lit the fuse.

She beat him and he ran upstairs. She walked to the front door and locked it from the inside. She threw the keys out the window and picked up a metal pipe that was sitting in a corner of the kitchen. For the next ten minutes, he begged her to stop. It was a balmy day and all the windows were open. The neighbourhood kids stopped playing to listen to my father's pleas. We were summoned upstairs and he sat on the bed's edge. His face was bruised and a stream of blood ran down the side of his head.

Go ahead, tell them you're sorry you called their mother a whore.

He couldn't face us and I was happy at seeing him hurt. He got a slice of what I endured. He brought me to her and now she turned her venom on him.

I'm so sorry. Please, forgive me.

The few lights in my life were my bonds with black girls. Unlike my kin, these strangers rallied around me. We rode our bikes and gossiped about classmates. We wondered aloud why our Dutch friends couldn't move their bodies. They taught me swear words in Papiamento, a Dutch version of patois. I was exposed to their fragrant and bright culture. One girl stood out in particular. Her family lived

upstairs from us. After arriving to the neighbourhood, she knocked on our door. Met by my stepmother, she asked if I could come out and play, but
since she didn't know my name, Samira presented
Isaac.

Not him, the other one!

I was called to the front door and she latched
onto my hand. We sat in the courtyard and she ran
her fingers through my hair.

I wish I had hair like yours.

I liked it when she pressed her nose against my
scalp and rubbed the palms of my hands.

How come your hands are so soft?

I kept smiling. If these things happened to me
as an adult, I'd assume she was in love with me. In
those juvenile moments, all that mattered was that
she thought my softness was beautiful. When I returned from playing, I was called into the kitchen.

That black girl is not to knock on my door again.

Being a willowy boy in a society that saw black
men and boys as aggressive was not easy.

Dutch girls appreciated the difference between
us and I needed their irrational fascination with my
somatic form. The first white girl I befriended lived
across from us with her mother and older brother.
Her parents divorced when she was young and her
father remarried. Her mother adopted a dog and

went about the thankless work of raising children. The girl's name was Anouk and she spoke about the divorce with such ease that it startled me.

I didn't understand how Dutch parents allowed their children to be privy to their business. In my culture, when adults discussed matters as grave as divorce, death, or unruly children, they dismissed the children from the room. The fact that the Dutch talked about their marital issues over breakfast, or had shouting matches over the kitchen island, was astounding. Despite these cultural differences, Anouk and I became fast friends.

As I entered the world of sexual exploration, stumbling blocks appeared. One of them was a Dutch girl named Saskia. She had just moved to the complex and wanted us to be more than friends. Unsure of how to explain my disinterest in girls, I asked for a week to consider. After a week, she duly returned.

Some white girl is here for you.

I was upstairs and opened the window to see who it was.

So, can we go steady?

She taught me how to French kiss and digitize pussy. It relieved my stepmother to see girls, although she viewed Dutch girls as loose, chasing after me. It meant that my mannerisms weren't an indication of what got me hard. As I got hot and heavy with Saskia, Yusuf courted Anouk. She came to me one day and asked if my friend had an interest in her.

He likes you a lot, actually.

Soon they too were going steady. Yusuf and I made it! We got ourselves some white bitches!

Yusuf and I got into devilish things together.

His hands were loose and I started fires. His lowest moment came when we were killing time at the mall. Videotapes were being phased out and DVDs becoming the preferred way of watching movies. They kept the DVD covers on the shelf and inserted the disc when you brought it to the counter. My poor friend didn't know this. He swiped an empty cover and ran out of the store, leaving me to fend for myself. I sauntered to the exit when I felt a firm grip on my collar. The hand led me outside.

Hey, we have your little friend. If you don't want him to go to jail, I suggest you come back.

He came to a halt and walked back with his head down. I was hurt that he had taken off without warning me. Later that evening, his sister collected him from the police station. Iron Eyes beat him so bad that he had a fever that night.

Violence was commonplace.

We were wounded people.

It was assumed we had the wherewithal to pick up where we left off. The rage of becoming dependents and the obscuring of our pain taxed our collective sanity. Violence was the expression of our frustrations. We were a proud people brought low by historical circumstance. No one had the time to figure out what went wrong because life had to go on. We had to thrive in this alien land and jealously guard whatever we had left of our culture. The Dutch, meanwhile, believed that the absence of violence, a Western education, and submersion in Occidental culture healed any spiritual kinks.

A neighbour of ours, a middle-aged Somali man nicknamed Rabbit, checked in on us from time to time. Samira cautioned us against letting in any adults when she was out. Fadumo, asserting her dominance in the absence of a parent, said he couldn't come in. Before she had a chance to close the door, he pushed his way in and beat her. I looked on from a distance. Here I, "the man of the house," was letting him knock my stepsister around. I imagined angels brought her low; but in reality, I had witnessed the abuse of a girl by a man who felt defied.

Another time Yusuf and I were riding our bikes around town on garbage day. The blue bins were uncovered and overflowing with paper products. Yusuf stole lighter fluid and a barbeque lighter. He rode ahead and poured it out as I followed with the lighter. The flames surged upward, seemingly from the sidewalk. The bins melted and residents doused the fires with water. We laughed at the havoc we had wreaked. The next day I returned to the scene of the crime. Sanitation workers were scraping the melted blue plastic off the sidewalk.

Have a nice day guys!

Over the years my class kept shrinking. By 1998, my final year at Bovenkruier, ten boys and five girls were left. I had a stormy relationship with two of the boys, Leandro and Pim. Leandro was the child of Antilleans. His ethnic ambiguity attracted Dutch children. He was black but not very dark, which intrigued them. Add to this his green eyes and they creamed their postmodern pants. His hair was curly, prompting comparisons between his and mine.

Pim was a Dutch boy with a stutter. He followed Leandro around like a lost puppy.

The trouble started with a bet. Leandro claimed he photocopied legal tender and used it in stores. I guffawed and he issued a bet for ten guilders, about seven Canadian dollars. As Monday rolled around, he came to class with a photocopy of a ten-guilder note. I was confused.

Pay me!

I reminded him that our bet was about whether he could use his counterfeit to pay. He shook his head and claimed it was about whether it was possible to photocopy money. This is when Pim, with his halting speech, started with threats. Adolescent boys have a pack mentality that can be haunting when you're the target. I fell out of favour with Leandro, and the other boys began to treat me like a leper. I was chosen last for teams during gym class. Our teacher had to force boys to talk to me when doing group assignments.

The girls in the class, though, were the salt of the earth. They guided me in the right direction. I was intrigued by beautiful garments and slick music videos.

Creativity was the way forward, but I didn't know what direction to take. Arts and crafts were not for me. I didn't sew well and my painting was imbecilic. When they asked me to choreograph their dance for the school talent show, I was elated. I had no friends among the boys so this was a way to escape social death in middle school. We assembled in the auditorium and I showed them the moves I picked up from girl groups and bad bitches in rap videos.

Sway your hips. Maintain eye contact with the audience. Step aside.

I showed them how I wanted it done.

Don't worry, you'll get it. Just keep at it.

I wasn't wanted at home. I wasn't welcome among the boys. These girls not only wanted my company but learned from me. They saw qualities in me that were denigrated by boys and my family. They showed me that being fierce wasn't something to be ashamed of.

This became the story of my life.

I wasn't welcome among the boys but the girls made room for me. My sarcastic attitude and pop-cultural knowledge were assets. None of them wanted to outdo me or challenge me to some physical activity. It was beauty that tied us. I wonder if they realized how they helped me?

I was on the verge of breaking down.

My teacher, who resembled a muscle daddy from a cheesy gay porno, didn't notice or care that I was being bullied. It got to a point where they openly threatened me in class. Words may sting, but they weren't a good reason to throw hands.

One day, while standing in line for a field trip, I poked one of the girls in the arm. She jokingly yelled. Before I knew it, Pim was in front of me, giving me the third degree. Why was he in my face? Was he watching me?

Fuck off!

He punched me in the gut and I blacked out. When I came to, his face was scratched up, his earring pulled out, and his blood flowed. I had bitten him in the cheek and drawn blood. Our teacher walked in to find this bloody mess and sent me to the principal's office.

I thought about killing myself more and more each day. I conjured up ways of doing it. I looked out the window of the bus and pictured my body splashed on the dark asphalt.

I ran into oncoming traffic. My body bounced from hood to hood.

J.G. Ballard would be proud.

How would Samira explain my death to my father?

I dreamt of him collecting my body for burial back home. Before he left, he stabbed her to death and set her corpse alight. Her disfigured body horrified her family, and in the next life, Satan turned her into his prized whore.

★ ★ ★

My stepsisters and Ismahan were three girls who didn't play around. If you upset them, they let you know.

Ismahan, in particular, wasn't blessed with patience. One day, she got tired of waiting for the door to be opened so she threw a brick through the back-door. I adored her sense of mischief and didn't ever think of reprimanding her. The antics of little black girls delighted me. If she jumped on the hood of a neighbour's car and shattered the windshield, I applauded it.

Let it out, baby!

One time my delight bent the antenna of a neighbour's car and when he asked for an apology, in lieu of payment, she cried.

How dare he!

Our eldest, Fadumo, was awkward and the effects of lockjaw left her with a lopsided smile. She got no love from the boys. They fawned over the plain-looking Dutch girls, who looked like crosses between beautiful mares and long-faced farmers.

Fadumo was also overshadowed by Ebyan and was well-behaved and did as she was told. As the eldest, she might have felt a sense of duty to show the rest of us how to be docile.

Ebyan, the middle one, made up for her lack of height with bravado and charisma. She got into fights and used to run away from home. One time, after she had been away for days, I found her hiding out in the bushes behind the house.

Warya, get me a sandwich. I'm so hungry.

I should've told her to starve, but I dutifully smuggled the sandwich back to her hideout.

With violence, its victims become its best practitioners. Despite the violence imposed on their bodies, my stepsisters joined their mother in tormenting me. I prepared for the day I'd strike back. I didn't know how the chance would present itself but I lived in a future of my own making. A showdown was inevitable, or so I thought.

Isaac and I didn't fight often, but once, we fought in the living room. I was chastised for crying, after he landed a punch to my face. I was assaulted as I woke up or walked through the door. Everything I said was a lie. My father, on one of his visits, beat me for coming home late because of a soccer game. He gave me a five-guilder coin. He saw fire in my eyes. Perhaps he felt he had gone too far. I was in pain all over because I was late from something they forced me to participate in. I thought about wiping them out.

Poison them? Set the house on fire? Just stab them.

Unabated rage roared within me. I was tainted by their violence, and the infection drove me to ponder mass murder.

The first time I stood up to the demons, I almost got stabbed.

Ebyan didn't like the noise Ismahan was making but she, as little girls are wont to do, didn't pay her older sister any mind. Ebyan slapped her across the face. I stepped between them.

Get out of the way, Mohamed. This doesn't concern you!

I wasn't going to let this heifer do my queen the way they did me. She wasn't going to fear us. Ebyan lunged at me. I pushed back. She ran over to the drawer and pulled out a knife. I grabbed one of the fake plants in the windowsill. I'd bash her face in with its concrete bottom. Fadumo ran to get Iron Eyes. The poor woman watched as this demon tried to snuff me out. No amount of screaming stopped her. If I was going to die, she'd spend the rest of her life being spoon fed and unable to speak. She, her fucking mother, this fucking country, haunted me. I wasn't safe from violence and intimidation anywhere.

Come on, bitch. Give it your best try.

The worst opponent is the kind who doesn't fear death. Years of blinding punches and ringing in my ears seeped all compassion from my bony frame. She realized I wouldn't retreat so she put the knife down.

It wasn't the last time one of my stepmother's kin lunged at me with a sharp object. Another incident began with an invitation to a birthday party. I asked for some money to buy a gift. Samira handed me a ten-guilder note and told me to buy sugar.

Use the change to buy a gift.

I got the sugar and hung the plastic bag on the handlebar. As I sped up, the bag got caught in the spokes and the sugar spilled everywhere. I panicked. I continued home and ran into Ebyan. She told me not to worry and to buy the present. I rode back to the mall and got a cheap red ball with black patches. When I got back, I explained what happened.

Isaac! Go see if there's any truth to what he's saying.

We rode in silence. I begged him to tell her he saw sugar on the ground. He refused. I rode back alone. I couldn't go to the party until I confessed.

I lied and told her I stole the money and never bought the sugar.

See, don't you feel better now that you told me the truth?

I smiled.

You can't go. You are a lying thief. I'm not going to reward you. Go and pray.

On Saturday, the day of the party, my classmate and his mother came to pick me up. I told them I couldn't go. Yusuf told me to break the rules.

Listen, what's the worst that could happen?

Since it was June, my allergies were in overdrive and a scavenger hunt in a freshly mown field didn't help matters. I tried to have a good time but my gut told me I was going to pay handsomely for defying the demon. I ate all the sweets I could and dipped chips in a tall glass of orange pop.

Samira was waiting when I got home from the party.

My eyes were throbbing because I had been rubbing them all afternoon. It was late and she told me to disrobe.

She struck me across the face. I closed my eyes. She readied the radio cord and a bowl of rice. The incense she had burned earlier hung in the air. I wondered if my real mother would hit me with such ferocity. I tried not to cry but the tears flowed. I imagined the next morning. She choked me, and when she let go, the rush of air left me in ecstasy.

Was I enjoying this?

She screamed insults at me. I kept crying. Next came the lashing. The first one hurt the most and successive ones were a relief. I knew the extent of the pain. The metal prongs dipped into my bloodied sweat. I kneeled on two mounds of rice. My hands, above my head, were on the wall.

In the story of Bilal, he's lashed by his master for refusing to denounce the Prophet Mohamed (peace be upon him). Tied to a boulder in the desert, he was left for dead.

I imagined the strength of Bilal. I was about to pass out, and blood stained the rice. The small of my back was drenched. She told me to keep kneeling until everyone got up in the morning. I tried. I slid into a slumber, on a bed of rice.

In the fall of 1998, I started junior high. The school, a giant Brutalist building, sat next to a park and an austere church. It was named William the Silent, after the founder of the House of Orange. His assassination at the hands of a Catholic stoked sectarian violence in the Netherlands. After his death, his Protestant followers attacked Catholic churches and purged them of "idols," which is what they called the holy statues and religious symbols inside them. That episode of Dutch history was referred to as Beeldenstorm, or Iconoclasm.

My own school history, though, became less violent. The bullying subsided. Yusuf and I spent more time together. He was in his second year at the same school. I became friends with some of the tough guys Yusuf hung around with. They passed me hashish cigarettes and we skipped class for mischief. My effeminate manner didn't matter as long as I went along with their antics. By this time, neither Yusuf nor I dated the white girls from the neighbourhood. He had moved on to more beautiful, ethnically ambiguous girls. They were nice but their personalities were very flat.

While Yusuf pursued pussy, I came across a real stunner. His name was Caspar and he was on the indoor soccer team with Yusuf. I watched them practise and Caspar's body moved with grace across the wooden floor. He had the qualities that drew the eye of a teenage queen. His bravado warmed my loins. His blond hair was made brighter by the sun. He took his clothes off within full view. I was unsure of what drove his exhibitionism but I took it all in. Unlike other Dutch boys, his dick wasn't a nuclear pink.

I couldn't shake him. He waited for me after class and bought me things. My little brain couldn't figure out he was courting me. Whenever he took out money, he insisted I stand beside him and watch the numbers. It was odd but I loved it. Once I knew I was desired, it gave me a sense of power. Caspar unlocked something in me that I wielded uncomfortably. I didn't know how to use it but I knew I had it. The sways of my lanky frame excited some men but repression didn't allow me to look them in the face. Instead, I lowered my gaze as their stares burned a hole in my pants.

At this time, I also took to squatting by the highway and pushing thick branches in my ass. I kept going until I bled. The drivers shot me disapproving glances as they whizzed past. I had no way of releasing the constant tension except by damaging my body. I felt alive only when in pain. The branches got thicker with each visit to the roadside. The blood made my underwear damp as I rode away, praying that any of the men walking their dogs or jogging would attack me. I'd pray that they'd rape me in the middle of the bushes. I fused my nascent sexuality with the violence I faced inside and outside the home.

No one ever answered my wish.

Unfortunately, I had no time to explore this relationship with Caspar because my stepmother announced we were moving again.

I was heartbroken.

I wanted to explore what it meant to love a body like my own but I lacked the courage to reciprocate. I wasn't brave enough to put my thick brown lips on his thin pink ones. I wanted to chew on his earlobe and bite his chin. I wanted his arms to envelope and pin me down but I wasn't brave.

I felt that whenever I got used to a place and the people around me, Samira was eager to shift locations. I didn't realize it then, but this is a tactic abusers use to keep their hostages isolated.

She wanted to control our connection to the outside.

We packed up and bid the small inter-riverine town farewell.

We moved to the deindustrializing city of Tilburg, in the south of the Netherlands. It was in the Catholic province of North Brabant. I was enrolled in a high school named after Catholic philosopher Cobbenhagen and located on a street named after Benjamin Britten. The whole neighbourhood was named after composers. We lived on Scarlatti. But I'm not sure if it referred to Scarlatti *père* or *fils*.

My classmates hailed from all over the world.

The number of Muslim students astounded me. Many of them were the children of *gastarbeiders*, or guest workers.

After World War II, the Netherlands imported millions of young Anatolian and Moroccan men to milk cows, pick fruit, collect waste, and do other jobs the *autochtoon*, or indigenous Dutchman, didn't care for.

I was one of few Somalis, but it was nice to be in the company of so many *buitenlanders*, or foreigners. The word *wallahi*, Arabic for "I swear in the name of God," was used with abandon.

Are you fasting?

Our teachers wished us a happy Eid. Despite the ubiquity of crucifixes, we were taught that all religions were equal.

I had no chance to explore friendships in my first year because of my careless mouth. I confided in a Moroccan classmate that I thought this one white boy in our class was a braggart, because he mentioned the expensive shit his parents bought him. During an arts and crafts class, the Moroccan boy yelled what I said to him across the room. After that day, the white boy and I became mortal enemies. It began a long year of bullying during which he and a cabal of demons made my school days a living hell.

During grammar class, he took me to the foot of the cross. The white boy threw pieces of paper at me. I threw them back.

You fucking idiot!

I chuckled.

Your nasty mom is an idiot.

He ran up and a shoving match ensued. The teacher flailed her arms around and implored us to stop. I was sent to the principal's office and broke down.

They won't leave me alone!

He marched me back into the class and admonished them. As I got ready to go home, I was told that the white boy was outside, waiting for me.

If he wanted a beating, he couldn't have picked a worse opponent. I got off my bike and got him to the ground. I pinned his neck between my knees and beat his back like a drum. I elbowed his neck as I drifted into a blackout. When we were pulled apart, his face was scratched up and his eyes full of tears.

He wasn't ready for this bitch.

★ ★ ★

I coped with a diminished sense of self by diving, headfirst, into the world of drugs. I smoked hashish with hoodlums. By age thirteen, I had moved on to pills.

The chemical name of my pill of choice was diazepam, otherwise known under its brand name: Valium. I was introduced to it by a classmate. On a sunny afternoon, he invited me to his place. I was in love with him, so I agreed. He had an air of superiority that was intoxicating. He rode a Porsche bike while mine was from a mail-order catalogue.

We rented a rowhouse in the vast proletarian hell between the industrial canals and the dairy farms.

His family owned a beautiful townhouse in the centre of town. His life seemed rich and full of love. I could tell that his mother cared about him because his lunches weren't leftovers or a cheese sandwich.

We made our way upstairs. He turned to me and asked if I'd try something. Here it was, I thought, my first encounter with his body. I had seen him naked in the change rooms and knew exactly where

I wanted to place my hands. When he returned from the bathroom with a bottle of pills, I was deflated.

My mom takes these to calm her nerves. Here, have one. Chew them up so they work faster.

I was in heaven. All worry washed away. I laid on the rug and chewed another. I asked him to bring me more the following day.

Before I knew it, I was taking them every day.

My stepmother thought an allowance was a way for white folks to spoil their children. So, I paid for these drugs by writing his reports. I didn't seem off, at first, so none of my teachers noticed my descent into hell. By the end of that school year, he was kicked out of school and I had no supply.

Over the summer, I got our doctor to write a prescription. In my second year at Cobbenhagen, I failed ten out of fourteen courses. The four I passed were Dutch grammar, history, English, and world religions. Science, math, and philosophy were not worth staying awake for. In the margins of my report card, my principal counselled my stepmother to seek medical help for me. She didn't read Dutch, so I told her it said I was sick too often during the school year. Withdrawal was a medical condition.

During my second year at Cobbenhagen I became friends with Selim. He was the son of Turkish immigrants who ran a furniture shop on the North

Ring Road. His hair was jet-black and his jeans tight, showing off his bubble butt. I was taken with him as soon as he sat down next to me. He had been held back a year and looked older than the rest of the boys, inspiring fear and commanding respect. He woke me from my Valium-induced naps by stroking my hair.

Selim introduced me to his friend Elson, who had also been held back. He was an awful student, despite the fact that his father taught science at the school. Elson's flirtations were more overt than Selim's. He sat close and whispered sweet nothings into my ear.

Mohamed, I think you're sweet.

His lips pressed against my ear.

Do you like me?

His warm breath burned me up. I wanted to grab his face and stick my tongue down his throat, but I was a coward. These boys wanted to do things to me, but I preferred thick branches by the highway. Elson was a beautiful boy whose parents were from the Antilles. His face betrayed generations of interracial fucking. He exuded a confidence and masculinity I wanted inside of me.

School work and learning the Quran took a backseat to pill popping and craving exotic boys.

I was overwhelmed and excited. The limits of my small-town upbringing were showing themselves. I used to be a token but now I was part of this giant, brown mass.

Islam wasn't avoided in this community. Previously, I'd felt uncomfortable with the sea of hijabs and the white kids miming our holy words. I'd felt at odds with my surroundings. I'd been fleeing from Islam.

But here, in the heart of Catholic Netherlands, it was on full display. It was the foundation of the school attended by Isaac and Ismahan. We went to Quranic classes at the community centre bordering the giant Ypelaarpark. I felt lifted, riding my bike through the park on my way to the Ringbaan Noord, or North Ring Road.

But Ebyan fucked it all up when she ran off to Toronto.

When the school year ended in that summer of 2000, I was also thrown out of Cobbenhagen.

Samira announced that we, like Ebyan, were moving to Canada. She was my stepmother's favourite. Whenever Ebyan ran off somewhere, we spent all evening on our bikes looking for her. Frantic phone calls to her friends' families kept Samira up well into the night. Ebyan's tall tales about where she had gone were accepted without question.

Canada? Where is that?

I showed Isaac where it was on the map.

America?

I shook my head and pointed to the slab of land sitting atop the United States.

THE GREAT WHITE NORTH

Paranoia as an African condition was written into the music of my soul. Fathers working abroad and mothers worrying that their husbands had a lover or, worse, a second wife. The neighbours were aunties but they couldn't see you slip.

Don't fuck up!

When such warnings were uttered in Somali, my body seized up. Paranoia about police, teachers, social workers, and other elements of the system. The fear of God was put in me when I learned what happened in the unbelievers' jails. Make friends but don't tell them what goes on at home. I was told to avoid Western culture, but absorb all the erudition it produced.

Pressure to do well heightened my anxiety. Photos of Brother Siad hung on the wall, but he was condemned for subduing a rebellious clan. The collective schizophrenia was intense but the bonds held, most of the time.

In Canada, I noticed that children of Trinis, Ghanaians, Ethiopians, and Jamaicans had the same concerns, with minor adjustments for cultural differences. Anxiety about being swallowed whole by antagonizing social forces.

The African, be they within or without Africa, furnished internal space with beauty and caution. A moment is nigh in which we, from Réunion to the South Side of Chicago, once again shall have a "Eureka!" moment.

I hope Kwame Nkrumah, a hero to all Africans, is holding hands with Malcolm X, Frantz Fanon, Nina Simone, and Miriam Makeba on the banks of heavenly streams.

BIENVENUE À TORONTO

On arrival in Toronto, I looked at the airport and took in the bland landscape around Airport Road. Years later, I discovered the blandness obscured countless strip clubs and steakhouses. In those unremarkable spaces, businessmen entered into deals and rewarded themselves with strippers and mountains of cocaine.

I felt a rush as we glided across the highway. The trucks avoided the barriers with mechanical grace.

My aunt picked us up in her purple Dodge Caravan, which I discovered was *the* Somali mode of private transport in the 4-1-6. This was Samira's sister who had waited for us at Heathrow back in 1991. She emigrated from the United Kingdom because of something that happened to a young girl, the child of a very religious family, in the care of my aunt. She left the child alone with her husband. The little girl returned home withdrawn and her family became worried. She revealed what happened. My aunt's husband had helped himself to her innocent body. Her family gathered at my aunt's house and threatened her husband. He happened to be out, perhaps ruining more lives. Molesting young girls was his real vocation. My aunt's family departed from the United Kingdom that night and resettled in Toronto, where he worked at a car-rental business at Pearson airport.

We pulled into Four Winds Drive, a desolate patch of North York. North York used to be its own city until it was forced into a marriage with Etobicoke, York, Scarborough, Old Toronto, and East York to form the megacity I had just landed in. Apparently, in Canada, cities are corporations owned by the province. Odd.

Her building was ten storeys high and near a giant oil plant, aptly named the Keele Street Tank Farm. On the other side of the building were a grassy field, hydro lines, and community gardens. Off in the distance were giant Brutalist blocks with long, metallic chimneys. I asked her what they were.

York. It's a university here. Isn't it ugly!

We huddled into the 1970s lobby of my aunt's apartment building. The walls were covered in mirrors. Upstairs we found my grandmother; my aunt's sons, one of whom had a lazy eye; her husband; and three cousins from Norway, daughters of Yasmin. Two of them were twins.

Phony hugs and kisses were exchanged.

Off in a corner was Ebyan. She acted like nothing happened. I hated her so much.

My first summer in Toronto was sweltering. The Petro-Canada at Sentinel Road and Finch Avenue West showed gas was going for forty-eight cents a litre, an astoundingly low price compared to the cost of fuel in Europe. Milk came in plastic bags and the aisles of the grocery stores had melted cheese in jars.

Everyone drove a huge car and my hay fever made the experience unbearable. I spent a lot of time indoors and was in awe of air conditioning, a North American comfort. My aunt had two microwaves. In the Netherlands, we used a conventional oven to reheat food. Every corner had a pizza shop or a convenience store. No one stopped me from looking at dirty magazines.

Are you going to buy that?

High-rises dotted the landscape in what was known as the "Jane and Finch area."

This area, if Toronto news outlets were to be believed, stretched from Jane Street and Steeles

Avenue West across to York University. It went as far south as Sheppard Avenue West.

If you walked it, you realized Jane and Finch isn't one homogenous neighbourhood. Suggesting it was reflected a view that when people of colour co-inhabited a part of town, they were a mass, much like the way referring to Africa as a whole, instead of its separate countries, is an infelicity.

The "area" suffered from the usual social ills associated with diverse and poor neighbourhoods. Every news outlet in the city identified one scourge or another.

Shooting at Jane and Finch building!
Baby falls from balcony!
Birthday party ends in stabbing!

The constant loop of bad news lost all meaning to me. The media kept sensationalizing and dissecting every act of violence that occurred in Jane and Finch.

My stepmother encouraged us to avoid *those black people*. I looked at her and wondered, which people? The people who lived the best way they could, despite the constant glare of police surveillance? The people who became my friends and classmates? What about them was so bad that I had to avoid them like the plague?

And when did we stop being black?

You see, they are not like us. They send their kids out on the street to be gangsters. Look at what's all over the news!

The media fed into this paranoia about the fear of darkness that Samira, as a Somali woman, always had. My stepmother was the kind of woman who abhorred darkness. She straightened her hair and bleached her skin with an assortment of creams from Asia.

The fear of darkness in Somali culture had many sources, both native and foreign. Its odious effects drove a wedge between those born or raised in Western cities with large populations of black Americans, Caribbeans, or Africans and the elders in our community. Somali youth aligned themselves, culturally and politically, with established black or African communities.

Proud Somali parents, including my own, saw this as a corruption of our Islamic values and long-held traditions. Suddenly, everything from opposing vaginal cutting to juvenile mischief was seen as an effort to corrupt our youth and the scapegoat, as per usual, were other black or African people.

The older members of the diaspora saw no value in the cultural output of black people in the Americas. They saw misguidance in their children resisting colonial relationships. We had to do well in school so that someday we could return to Somalia to rebuild. In essence, we forewent any sense of self in our new homes so that we might go back and fix a country they fucked up in the first place.

I wanted to explore the neighbourhood alone but was stopped by my aunt.

If you need to go somewhere, I will drive you.

The furthest I went was to Fountainhead, the giant park in front of her complex.

I'm not sure if the park's planner hated humanity or loved Ayn Rand or both.

Groups of brown kids played cricket. Somali mothers watched their kids dangling from the monkey bars and judged uncovered Somali girls on their way to Yorkdale Mall.

I came across a public pool where children splashed each other. Overseeing the hectic joy was always a tanned white boy or girl wearing red shorts and a tank top. I stood by the fence and took deep breaths of the chlorinated air. I decided against joining them. I didn't know how to have healthy fun.

THE PAST IN PICTURES

As summer faded into autumn I settled into my new high school, up the street from Four Winds, named C.W. Jefferys.

Apparently, it had been named after Charles William Jefferys, a painter of martial kitsch. He had emigrated from England in the nineteenth century and aided our future by putting Canada's European past in pictures.

I was shown around the building by the principal.

You speak English so well!

Her smile was unsettling. Its permanence bordered on the plastic. I didn't realize it then, but smiling was something of a pastime in this country. Smiling in the Netherlands was akin to a crime.

I was taken to a portable classroom and introduced to the English teacher. She was a few months away from giving birth. I sat down in the back of the class. I looked out onto the road and made peace with the fact that Toronto was my new home.

The Somali is a wanderer. In this postmodern world, our stops at the oasis included monstrosities like Toronto.

The school had been built for the children of the socially mobile white workers of the post-war era; although, the changing faces in the graduation pictures lining the hallway between the exit and the office showed white flight at work.

Mind you, it wasn't just Anglos who fled the area in droves but also the children of Italian immigrants. Many of them started families in Woodbridge, Concord, and Maple, Ontario. They were replaced by the children of West Indian immigrants who arrived in huge numbers thanks to Trudeau *père*. The children of Sino-Vietnamese, Tamils, Somalis, West Africans, and the occasional Eastern European soon joined them.

The quality of the school went down as the tax base declined. The Toronto District School Board's operation ensured social and economic disparities between its students. Each district within Toronto funded schools based on the property taxes levied in that area. If homeownership was low, the tax collection was lower.

Since most of the housing stock in the Jane and Finch neighbourhoods consisted of rental housing, it was classed as commercial, bringing lower revenue to the schools in the area. This was reflected in the yearly threats of pool closures, fewer school trips, dissolving books, and teachers who made due with what was available.

Since our student body was overwhelmingly of colour, many teachers saw their role primarily as government-paid babysitters for a bunch of unruly savages. It was common for guidance counsellors to discourage students from taking academic courses or applying to universities. One cannot imagine a guidance counsellor in the tonier, whiter High Park or Forest Hill districts of Toronto telling students to give up their dreams of going to university and pick up a trade.

The relationships between the white teaching staff and the largely brown and black student body prepared many of us for the cruel reality of a racist society and the undermining of our abilities.

The school was different from what I had experienced in the Netherlands. No longer was there pressure to assimilate since there was no discernible Canadian culture to speak of. Instead, we were encouraged to remain loyal to the culture from whence we came. I saw the nobility in this undertaking, but what were you to do if you came from a place that had essentially imploded on itself?

I was taken from my motherland at the age of four and spent the greater part of my youth trying to be Dutch. Now that I was in the frigidity of the Great White North, I was expected to revert to a culture I had abandoned. This cluelessness about how to be a Somali didn't win me any Somali friends at school.

The young Somalis in the area opted to become "black." They too had forsaken their own culture, but in favour of black American or West Indian culture, as opposed to my assimilation into Dutch culture.

They spoke Jafaican and dressed no differently from youths in Baltimore or Detroit. At home it was Islam and *anjeero* for breakfast, while outside it was beef patties and hip hop. This duality came at an existential cost.

You're not really black.

I didn't understand the thunderous truth behind those mocking words.

What did we know of the pain of having ancestors taken from Africa and sold like beasts of burden to the highest bidder? What did we know about the trauma of children being separated from mothers because whites needed free labour to pick cotton, mine gold, or cut sugarcane? What did we know about building a whole new culture from scratch?

What did we know about hiding from hooded men riding around at night? What did we *really* know about that?

The truth was, very little. Instead, within the Somali community we ignored our complicity in the Indian Ocean slave trade. And I, meanwhile, used the suffering of the rest of the black community in Toronto to shelter myself from the loss of my own culture and home.

It wasn't noble, but I was a maggot, feeding on the entrails of my fellow citizens' hospitality.

During my first year in Toronto certain things became apparent.

Unlike in the Netherlands, public transit was lacking. The city's spatiality wasn't conducive to walking. Long stretches became a desert, devoid of foot traffic. My stepmother learned how to drive. We used to get on our bikes, but one can't ride a bike with certainty in Toronto. Not even pedestrians were safe from drivers. What made drivers so upset? In Canada, the water was clean, every other business had a drive-through, and they controlled most of the built streetscape, yet they were full of rage.

In January of 2001, we moved to a blue and white building along Lawrence Avenue West, next to the

Black Creek expressway. It was nicknamed Vietnam for the fights and gunplay that happened there. The building was a dystopian Tower of Babel. We were crammed into units containing two or three bedrooms. The smell of meals being prepared seeped through walls and I found myself walking into a screen of fish curry every time I entered the hallway or bathroom.

The building's superintendent was a sharply dressed woman from El Salvador. She informed us, gleefully, that we were in a unit previously occupied by her niece and her niece's boyfriend. I wish she had told the niece to throw out her blood-soaked tampons so I didn't have to.

The head of security happened to be the superintendent's brother. She ran quite the family operation!

In touting her family's cohesion, she couldn't have foreseen her son fighting her brother in the parking lot behind the building, for all to see. It was quite the spectacle and I watched the whole thing while devouring a Boston cream doughnut.

Another thing I noticed was Toronto's racial segregation. Most of the teachers at C.W. Jefferys were white, but none lived in the vicinity of the school or near any of us.

The towers lining Finch housed thousands of souls who struggled to make it in the Great White North. Their travails went unnoticed.

We knew better than to hang out at a particular corner for too long lest the boys in blue came through. I was more concerned about the police than the criminals or gun violence. They rode up and down the neighbourhood and made their presence felt. Toronto's motto is *diversity is our strength*. What is more diverse than black flesh on a police baton!

Diversity was a lovely sideshow to distract us from the mouldy walls in the buildings. There was nothing diverse about books falling apart in neighbourhood schools or seeing young men stopped and carded. Diversity was a ploy to gloss over the obscene disparities in this supposed just and free society.

But all that rhetoric was put on hold because the psychopathic child of a Saudi billionaire was about to upend it all.

It was the second Tuesday in September and started like any weekday did. I got ready for school and boarded a northbound Jane bus to Finch. It wasn't until the second period that a classmate rushed into our portable classroom and announced that a plane had flown into the World Trade Center in New York City.

I thought it was a sick joke until a voice came on over the PA system. We were told to stay put until further notice. The voice was cracking and a slow panic swelled up. Twenty minutes later, another voice came on over the PA. A second airplane had flown into the towers. We were dismissed for the day. We were to go directly home since no one knew if Toronto was a target.

Nothing on that day prepared me for the new ways of the world. Being a Muslim became a social liability. The mundanity that made North America desirable turned to face us with its hideous side. The America of my dreams was soap operas, commercials, hip hop, fast food, endless highways, and fashion. American violence entertained me for hours. Now violence came to the mecca of capital. Human bodies tumbling from burning skyscrapers was no longer Hollywood melodrama; it was the stuff of the evening news. Images of the towers collapsing, like police killings of black people today, were played on a constant loop. The media worried that in the new millennium, we might forget.

I found my youngest aunt, Yasmin, in the living room. In the Middle East, she had cooked, cleaned, ironed our school uniforms, and made us little treats.

Did you hear what happened to America?

I sat beside her. I asked her where her sister was.

She's buying a car. I bet you, it was those Jews. Israel is behind this.

I turned to her.

I'm sure it was one of us.

She insisted that it was an inside job, or Jews, or both. I had no energy to keep arguing with her and offered her some tea. Being named Mohamed stopped being fun from that day on.

I wasn't taught that it was *halal* to fly planes into buildings. No one at our mosque suggested we strap bombs to ourselves.

There was a story about one of the Prophet's early followers. He was mortally wounded in battle. He implored the Prophet to let him kill himself. The Prophet said that his service to Allah would be undone by his suicide. Suicide, our elders warned us, was the greatest sin.

After the attacks I became more aware of my faith.

Does Islam hate freedom? Does your mother dress like a ninja?

I wanted to be like my Canadian friends, but nothing I said changed their minds. Islam, to many of my friends, was the faith of radical black Americans, crazed Arabs, and the Indians they grew up

with in the Caribbean. They had no concept of Somali Sufism or of the ecstasy induced in the bodies
of dervishes twirling and twirling.

I decided to try another tack and instead of being noticeably Muslim, I avoided all talk of Islam. I
went from Mohamed to Mo. During the month of
Ramadan, I ate hamburgers with my friends.

September 11, 2001, gave birth to "ex-Muslims."
A prominent one was Ayaan Hirsi Ali. She was a
Somali woman who served as a parliamentarian in
the Netherlands. She was a perfect warrior for the
West in the "War of Ideas." Her father had opposed
the Barre regime and she had spent her youth in
Nairobi, attending prestigious schools and em-
bracing revolutionary Islam. She claimed to have
burned a copy of *The Satanic Verses* and apologized
to Salman Rushdie for doing so.

A little much if you asked me.

She was married off to a young man in Toronto and on her way to join him, she ran away to the
Netherlands. Her refugee blues were similar to the
lies my stepmother told. These tall tales came back
to haunt her. She became an advocate for battered
immigrant women and against misogyny in Muslim
communities in the Netherlands. She morphed into
an effective mouthpiece for those spreading "democracy" in Muslim lands.

I wanted to cause confusion, and contrarianism allowed me to look at things differently. If Islam was a refuge for my family, my back was turned to it. Where they saw spiritual calm, I saw desert barbarism. The events of 9/11 were a "get out of jail free card." I was content to let Western media do the talking for me, but the contrarian in me objected to how they portrayed Muslims. Only I had the inalienable right because Islam had abused me. I bad-mouthed the *deen*, or faith, but gave ex-Muslims the side-eye. They were pimping out their experiences whereas I had a legitimate gripe.

The North American school experience was not what I expected. The student body didn't mesh with the imagined realities I had consumed in the Netherlands. Televised images were more real than the reality I was in. I craved the televised utopia of white faces.

Every morning the national anthem marked the beginning of the day. We rose and sang along. I had heard the Dutch anthem only when the national soccer team was playing. Flying the tricolour was acceptable only for national holidays, but in Toronto, the maple leaf flew above homes, malls, highways, schools, hospitals, government offices, on the backs of cars, and so on. The thing seemed to be everywhere.

In the Netherlands, nationalism had wiped out Jews, communists, homosexuals, Jehovah's Witnesses, black people, and the Roma. No one was eager to sing *Wilhelmus van Nassouwe, ben ik van Duitse bloed*. Canada, on the other hand, seemed gung-ho about pushing its vision of the Great White North on the *buitenlanders* entering its urban landscape from Victoria to Halifax.

My favourite course in school always involved a language. In the Netherlands I read a novel entitled *Boris*. It recounts the story of a young boy named Boris in Leningrad. His mother grew weaker with each passing day. His friend Natasha heard of a plot of land just outside the city where they could find some potatoes. They braved the Nazi lines and the bitter cold. They crossed a lake, which appeared frozen. One of them fell in and was saved—by a German soldier! He let them return home. In the end, Boris appreciated the kindness of the Aryan soldier. No mention was made of the Nazis taking twenty million of his fellow countrymen. These were the sort of stories I was fed in Dutch schools. Little did I know how horrible this indoctrination was; then again, I saw nothing wrong with Zwarte Piet—Black

Peter—until I told a West Indian friend in Toronto about it.

Every year, around the beginning of November, the Dutch celebrate the impending arrival of Saint Nicholas of Myra, or Sinterklaas, to towns and villages across the flat terrain. He comes bearing gifts for those who've been good, and his "helpers" take the naughty children back with him. His "helpers" are grown men and women in blackface.

The story goes that Saint Nicholas, an early saint from what is today Turkey, once heard a widower lamenting his inability to secure a dowry for his daughters. Saint Nicholas scaled the roof of the house at night and threw gold coins down the chimney. The widower awakened to find his prayers answered.

Myth has it that the roof-scaling Saint Nick had a black servant with him that night. This part of the myth was conjured up in 1850 by a schoolteacher named Jan Schenkman, who became a kind of Dutch Charles Dickens in helping establish modern Christmas traditions in the Netherlands.

Although the Dutch abolished slavery in 1863, the invention of a black servant for the gift-bearing saint tied blackness, in the minds of millions of Dutch children, to servitude.

Zwarte Piet, the modern and thoroughly racist interpretation of the saintly servant who turns up all over the Netherlands during the holidays, supposedly got black from the soot in the chimney. But I don't think soot is the reason for the woolly hair, large red lips, and gold earrings Peter's stand-ins wear in a typical Dutch Christmas parade.

A PLACE OF NO ABIDING USE

Stories are one of the few Somali art forms that have survived into the present day. When a home was packed up and loaded onto a camel, there was no need for wall decorations. Anything lacking a purpose was neglected. Our creativity, as a people, rested entirely on our tongues. Instead of family portraits or calligraphic tiles, we had the lore of ancestors, heroic tales, and the travails of roaming holy men. Poetry sneaked into every aspect of life.

In the Netherlands, it was difficult to attend many Somali events since the community was so dispersed. By the time we moved to Toronto, Samira had found a videographer's business that rented out tapes of weddings.

In them were women referred to as poetesses who recited the long and proud traditions of the two clan families being united.

They paused their recitations so the women could perform *buraanbur*, a dance in a circle.

The idea was to do it in a stylized but unique way. The poetess beats a drum and ululation rang throughout. My stepmother rented these videos and pointed out who she knew and suspected of gaining weight.

A bad habit I picked up from fellow students was the use of outdated language. I was so invested in mimicking West Indians, I adopted their verbiage. It came to a head during a sociology course taught by a child of Korean immigrants. She had gone to Queen's University in Kingston, Ontario. She was living the Canadian dream, white husband and all. As I sat in the back of the classroom, the young ladies around me discussed lunch.

Yo, let's go to that Chinaman place in the plaza.

Our teacher ran across the room and slammed her hand, palm down, on my desk.

Mohamed, you will not use such foul language. You understand!?

All eyes were on me as I struggled to lift my head. I nodded and she returned to the front of the room. She thought that I, as a child of African refugees, should know the sting that came with racist language. I hadn't considered any of that, to be honest. I wanted to impress the girls with my Jafaican attitude.

I pilfered from one marginalized group to insult another.

I was filled with regret about my words, so I raised my hand whenever questions were asked. I volunteered to hand out exams and collected assignments. In an effort to flatter me, our teacher commended me.

I'm happy to see you're not like the rest of them.

I was so proud of myself. I thanked her.

I formed a close relationship with one of the young ladies in that class. Her name was Tamika and her parents had moved to Toronto from Clarendon Parish in Jamaica. They were educated people and her mother insisted she not speak in anything accented by patois. Her mother insisted she move away from her culture, even as I was cautioned about straying too far from mine.

They liked it when she spoke in the flat tones of the Great Lakes region. She fascinated me with her willingness to talk sex and everything that came with it. She was dating the brother of one of our classmates and regaled me with the bullshit of their tryst. She knew I was a homosexual but made little effort to broach the subject. We lacked the language to communicate properly about buggery.

As we settled into our life of solitary confinement beside the expressway, my stepmother sought out Quranic schools in the area. We attended a mosque named Khalid Bin Al-Walid, but after the towers in Manhattan came down, the mosque was besieged with bomb and death threats.

Someone recommended a class in one of the buildings on the corner of Dixon Road and Kipling Avenue. The area around the buildings was home to a large Somali community and was known in the tabloid press, rather pejoratively, as Little Mogadishu.

The teacher at Quranic school was a sadist. He was a heavy-set man who grew an uneven beard and wore leather socks. We paid $75 per month for each of us. There were about thirty other kids in the class. He relished our tears. When we made a mistake, he ordered a fellow student to retrieve a switch from a tree outside and then used it on the offender.

To avoid such a beating, I once recited perfectly the whole of the Quran's first chapter, known as Juz 'Amma. My little sister, Ismahan, memorized it by age six or seven. I wasn't able to do it until I was seventeen.

I began to rebel, quietly and passively, against the Islamizing nature of my family. It was a middle finger to their hypocritical faces. I was sick of knowing that my family was on good terms with my aunt's husband, a known child molester. I was sick of pretending to love and cherish them, although they were not my real relations. I was sick of being blamed for everything that went wrong. No longer was my conscience playing this charade.

In *Somalia: Nation in Search of a State*, the historian Samatar discusses the two currents that were at the centre of Somali culture. The first was an intense loyalty to family and the larger clan around it. The second current was the fierce independence rooted in nomadic journeys, which was the one that intrigued me most.

I was ready for the journey but where would I go? How would I get there? How would I leave the only family I knew?

Fear must haunt every nomad at the beginning of a journey.

Eventually, I'd reach an oasis. My journey was about understanding myself and how we as a people morphed into one state of being and abandoned others.

Abandoning yourself to wear the clothes of another was a pastime for two white brothers I went to school with. They were skinny and something of a laughingstock. People called them "wiggers," which they relished. Being black was what they craved the most. They sagged their pants lower than any of the black boys in school. Their shirts consumed their tiny white bodies whole. I never understood kids like that. They were the beneficiaries of imperialism yet here they were miming people who reinvented themselves at every turn.

A lot of minority youth did the same thing, but the difference was that white boys in urban dress were not seen as criminal.

It was not the clothes that made authority figures uncomfortable. It was the levels of melanin in their skin. Since they lacked the key ingredient, they excelled at being black in different ways. They wrote lame rhymes and battled anyone on the sidewalk in front of the school. It was sad but they had the time of their lives. Playing dress-up with black culture was a prerequisite for white male adulthood.

My first foray into storytelling was in Grade 10. It was for an English course taught by a child of Eastern European immigrants. In that story, I referred to the depth of someone's hair colour as "oily black," which my teacher corrected to "jet black."

As part of our final writing assignments, we read a novel and wrote an essay about it. She brought me a title from the choices on the assignment sheet. It was *The Power of One* by Bryce Courtenay. He was a white South African writer who lived in Australia.

It told of a child raised by a Zulu mammy on a Boer estate. As the boy nursed on the repressed history of his nursemaid, he had vivid dreams, of the automaton kind fashionable among Surrealists. In one of them, the farmer's child dreamt he was Shaka Zulu.

I didn't understand the anger I felt then but I can vocalize it now. It was a poisonous book. The child nourished from the African woman's body in order to inhabit her history. The child, wealthy and white, is then adorned with the crown of a black king who died resisting colonial advances. The child is the white future feasting on the trounced black past of South Africa.

These reflections, rather youthful and incomplete at the time, collided with the blossoming of my sexual nature. Being a bibliophile was a wonderful cover. I read erotic novels and looked at Leni Riefenstahl's photos of South Sudanese tribesmen. I didn't grasp how quickly Hitler's cinematic propagandist had gone from worshipping Aryan zest to documenting African grace. Nothing Riefenstahl produced competed with the Internet. It had hours of pornography of every variety. I sought out porn involving black booties doing battle with black dicks.

During these searches I was introduced to the realm of interracial gay sex. Its pervasiveness astounded me. It was a mission to find men like the ones in my environment without the porn involving a white body. The theme was always the same: a poor white queen in distress who had no choice but to give up his shaved booty to throngs of black dicks. The thugs alluded to in the titles didn't refer to the white bottom. I knew who the thug was. If we weren't criminals, we were seducers who excelled, far more than the white producers of the film, in the art of sex.

Europeans didn't know of sub-Saharan Africa until the Portuguese sailed around the Cape of Good Hope. The imagined dominance of black bodies, skin, and "blood" was something that can be laid at the doorstep of Greco-Roman colour symbolism. It was rooted in the Greek and Roman association of death, misfortune, and ill-omen with the colour black.

By imbuing the colour with sinister meaning, they transferred those views onto the African form. Herodotus, during his time in Egypt, wrote about topless dancers on riverboats along the Nile. Liberated dark breasts offended his sense of propriety.

In Pliny, the African ceased to be human and morphed into a monster. We were creatures who used oat straws to drink because we had only one orifice on our faces. Those ideas were absorbed into a nascent Christianity and provided us with lovely nuggets of black mischief. According to the ascetic and hermit Saint Anthony, the devil came to him in the form of little black boys and girls, eager to defile him. He was setting a trend for the priests of the future Church.

The early Islamic caliphates brought translated versions of lost Greco-Roman classics back to Europe. Arabs, before becoming Muslims, had their own fanciful ideas about why black flesh was so evil, filthy, and useful for nothing more than servitude. When asked about the unity between black and Arab Muslims, many point to Bilal, an African slave who was one of the earliest followers of Prophet Mohamed (peace be upon him).

The idea that black flesh is violable and to be used as one pleased pervaded many Arab lands. Eventually, these ideas found confluence in the home of Christopher Columbus. The Europeans in North America gave these pernicious views about dark skin a whole new meaning. Black Americans converted to Islam because they thought it lacked the racist history of Christianity. In the Americas,

Islam may not have been a contributor to the idea of the African as a monster, but if they scratched the surface a little deeper, it became clear that Abrahamic faiths viewed darkness as evil and lightness as the imprint for God's innocence on Earth.

Thinking about histories was taxing, so I shifted to the here and now. Fashion was a great escape from all these existential concerns. At the beginning of the millennium, we looked to the American rap and Jamaican dancehall scenes to see what was going on.

A major roadblock to imitating those styles was a lack in the coins department. Samira didn't consider fashionable clothing an essential. I wanted to look fly in my last year of school. In the summer of 2002, I landed a summer job at an amusement park north of the city.

That same summer, I went to summer school at Bathurst Street and Finch Avenue West. The area was largely Jewish and most of the students spoke Russian. The course I took was an introduction to Canadian government. I listened, in the sweltering heat, to an indifferent teacher and endured the Russian-accented debates the Jewish kids got into with him. The bus ride to work, up Bathurst, took me past lawns plastered with signs that read Water for Israel. I was amazed by the uniformity of it all. Religion married nationalism in Canada and became lawn furniture.

I was a cashier at the amusement park. I spent several days a week in a kiosk and stole a few thousand dollars over the course of the summer. I lost that job before the season's end but it was for tardiness. My supervisor called home. As I listened to her diatribe, I saw her face turn. I was free to go. Apparently, Fadumo told them that I hated their guts and that they were doing me a favour by letting me go.

My need for money was unceasing so I found another job, my first at a call centre. We called unsuspecting Americans and offered them "zero interest" credit cards. All the credit card numbers were printed on sheets of A4 paper, along with the activation codes.

I didn't go back after my first shift because it seemed shady. A few weeks later I tuned into the evening news. I saw Mounties raiding the place and dragging the man who hired me past the thirsty cameras. I laughed even louder when I found out my schoolmates stole the sheets of paper and were ordering clothes and sneakers over the Internet. Bless them and their wily ways.

That school year I lost two classmates. Both were Tamil, and their families had fled the civil war in Sri Lanka between the Sinhalese government and the Liberation Tigers of Tamil Eelam. The first who died wore baggy clothes and giant necklaces. I'm sure his parents worried about him forsaking their ancient culture for the glossy shit we hankered for. All that aside, he was always jovial and cracking lewd jokes. One night, while out with friends, they encountered a foe of theirs and a drag race ensued. He was in the back and didn't have his seat belt on. When the car came to a screeching halt, he flew through the windshield. On the cold asphalt, in the free world of Toronto, a child of Tamil Eelam bled out. When it happened, his parents were probably working their second jobs so he and his siblings could have a better life.

The second one perished under entirely different circumstances. This young man was a bit nerdier than the first and a hopeless romantic. I was elated when a transfer student responded to his cheesy poems and proclamations of undying love. Most people didn't understand how colourism in South Asian cultures works. At the top of the social ladder are the lighter-skinned northerners. At the bottom are the Tamils and other dark-skinned groups such as the Dalits, or Untouchables. My friend invested too much in the lie of Toronto's diversity. The young woman's parents, predictably, demanded she stop seeing him. When he offered to meet them, they declined. He became despondent and leapt to his death in the name of love.

Nowadays, when a student dies, grief counsellors are made available. But at that time, our wonderful educators never mentioned it. They figured death was a normal part of our dark lives. Years later, a student named Jordan Manners was shot on the steps where I hung out. His mother was photographed, wailing on a patch of grass near a bus stop. Our grief mattered only if the white gaze consumed it.

In my Grade 12 English class the young white teacher introduced us to a short story set in Barbados. I forget the title, but before we read it, she handed out pieces of sugar cane. She wanted us to taste the sweetness that had claimed so many black lives. After we finished the story, she asked us to put together a proposal about what books we would like to write essays about. Armed with the taste of sugar cane, I made my way to the York Woods library. I asked where they kept the black writers and spent the next few hours figuring out which one I enjoyed the most.

I settled on Richard Wright. Wright was born in the inland port city of Memphis, Tennessee. When he was a little boy, he set his family's house on fire. His mother and younger brother moved in with his maternal grandmother. His father vanished from sight. The two years it took for me to discover Wright was a testament to the education I received.

Teachers pushed bullshit like Courtenay's *Power of One* instead of Wright's masterful *Black Boy: American Hunger*. Wright became aware of Jim Crow when he rode his bike one day. Behind were the stalking hands of aimless white youth. They pulled up beside him and acted friendly. Suspecting nothing, the young Wright reciprocated by continuing the small talk. Before he knew it, one of them had him by the scruff of the neck while the driver accelerated. He was dragged along this desolate dirt road and left bloodied. The helplessness he felt wasn't something I could imagine, but not for a lack of trying.

When we moved to the Netherlands, my siblings and I regularly ran from groups of skinheads eager to kick our heads in with their steel-toed boots. This wasn't an everyday occurrence and we teamed up with other *buitenlanders* to beat them.

Such recourse wasn't available to Wright as a young boy or as a grown man. The black American learned to accommodate the white spectre. Wright persevered and became active in radical politics. He joined the Communist Party, one of the few political parties that welcomed black Americans. He moved to Chicago and wrote his magnum opus, *Native Son,* there. He was a guest of Kwame Nkrumah in independent Ghana. Wright renounced his communist beliefs in 1944, in an essay that was published in *The Atlantic Monthly* and later included in a series of essays by other ex-communists entitled *The God That Failed*. His lasting contribution was his tutelage of the legendary James Baldwin.

As I got lost in the splendour of the written word, Samira was due for another sojourn in the Middle East. She left us in the care of my two stepsisters while she spent the winter months bathing in the Gulf of Aden or eating fried fish on the Abu Dhabi corniche. She never brought us back what we asked for and shrugged when we pointed this out. Fadumo and Ebyan hosted friends for sleepovers, went out on Friday nights, and ate like Americans. The menu consisted of frozen lasagnas, buckets of fried chicken, and cheeseburgers.

By this time, the Winter Olympics in Salt Lake City were underfoot and we had moved back to Four Winds Drive. I was writing a report on chromosomes for my biology class. The computer was in my stepsisters' room so I quietly typed away as they and their friend slept off their nighttime antics.

A knock at the door presented my aunt, the one married to the child molester. She pushed past me. She woke the girls and berated Ebyan and Fadumo. I kept writing my dry report on Gregor Mendel and his peas. She demanded I leave the room. I explained that I was working on an assignment worth a quarter of my final grade. She didn't care and I didn't budge.

Next thing I knew, she struck me. I got up and pushed her. She scratched my face and pulled my hair. The girls intervened, but she attacked them. My eldest aunt came in and screamed at us. The predator's wife ran to the kitchen and grabbed a knife. She lunged at me and missed. The nonsense didn't die down until my eldest aunt's husband came in and demanded the grown women leave the apartment. He reminded them that Samira had entrusted the two girls with looking after me and my younger siblings, yet here my aunt was trying to stab me. His wife wasn't having it.

Out of all the aunts, the eldest was the only barren one. As a result, we greeted her first, unless my grandmother was in the room; then, she was second. Her younger sisters deferred to her because they felt pity toward her. I'm not sure if this was apparent to her, because she lorded over them just the same. She began yelling at her husband. He walked away from her.

If you leave, that is it for the two of us.

In the hallway that morning, she lost her husband.

He called her bluff and disappeared into the snowy streets of Toronto. They eventually reconciled, but the man had backbone, unlike the other men married to these evil sisters. The remaining three sisters were married to sexual predators, philanderers, or bums. He was the exception. He was musically gifted, and it made him relatable to an awkward teen.

As I developed more into a man, some curious things happened. I noticed evenly spaced bumps around the head of my penis. I researched sexually transmitted diseases online and I became convinced I had genital herpes.

I asked Tamika about this and she told me that in order to contract an STD, I needed to have sex first.

My stepmother was always obsessed with my weight. I wasn't gaining any and she dragged me to the doctor's office and demanded a sonogram. The doctor was taken aback and after a few simple questions determined I was in tip-top shape. Still, my stepmother insisted on the sonogram.

On the day of the exam, I made my way east along Finch to Keele. Catholic schoolgirls in their uniforms were catcalled as they crossed the street. When I got to the sonogram office, a room full of pregnant women and their sperm donors met me. I hid behind a baby magazine and when my name was called, I jumped up and scurried away from their probing stares.

The examiner asked me to take my shirt off and applied a cold gel. He ran the wand up and down my belly and at times got uncomfortably close to my crotch. There wasn't anything out of the ordinary. I asked him to put this in writing, and he gave me a funny look.

Mohamed has no worms eating his food.

The only sure thing in my life then were my friendships with the daughters of West Indian immigrants like Tamika. I felt close to her because both of us were trying to get away from our family's religious fundamentalism. She belonged to a sect of Protestants called Seventh-Day Adventists. Like some Jews, they fasted from sundown Friday to sundown Saturday. They attended church all day Saturday until it was time to return home and break the fast.

She didn't care for religious formalism, but I remember how excited she got about choir practice. Had I known at the time that she was fucking the pastor's son, I would have understood why she was so happy about going.

In an effort to push back against the moralizing nature of our non-African religions, we talked about raunchy sex, bondage, and fantasies. Her first serious boyfriend was the brother of our friend Monique. It was so cool that she was able to net a guy in his early twenties. She knew how to exploit her sexual prowess and I was eager to learn. I wanted to tempt men, especially West Indian ones.

Whenever women asserted their sexual freedom in the way men did, they were denounced or looked down upon. A man was patted on the back, but a woman who let a dick enter her, outside the confines of marriage, was a whore.

Tamika helped me understand this so clearly. I knew women were treated differently but I lacked the lived experience to undergird this suspicion. The tension arising from her sexual liberation and membership in a conservative congregation were exciting to her.

As we neared the end of our high school careers, she told me a disturbing story. These days, sexual harassment and rape are talked about a lot more openly.

What was her part?

Why was she there?

The fact that she was sexually liberated kept her silent.

People will tell me that I had it coming. I shouldn't have been flirting with him, really.

The story began with a fellow classmate, a boy. He was on the basketball team and was never without cornrows and a gym bag. He showed a great interest in our conversations about sex and sexuality and we invited his two cents. Nothing about him seemed off and we treated him like a friend. He didn't live in our neighbourhood but when he offered to walk us, I didn't think anything of it. I left them at Finch and Sentinel and made my way to Four Winds. When they got to her building, he asked to use the bathroom. When they got upstairs, she pointed him down the hall.

I don't want to walk into the wrong room. Can you show me which door it is?

She was about to turn on the lights in the bathroom when he grabbed her hand and placed his flaccid penis in it. They stood there and she pulled her hand away. She took a seat in the living room and left him in the bathroom. As he made his way to the front door, he flashed her one more time. As she was recounting this, she had a slight grin on her face.

His dick was so fucking small!

We stopped referring to him by his Christian name and instead called him Shorty Poop-Stick. He became *persona non grata* and any attempt at conversation from him was met by laughter. He knew we thought his dick was inconsequential and not the sort of thing we liked inside us.

I wonder how such brazen displays of sexual aggression affected my friend?

The thing with the girls at C.W. Jefferys was that they couldn't afford to show vulnerability, or weakness as they would have it. Sexual violence of that variety was common because of the silence that surrounded it. What I saw were wounded spirits incapable of verbalizing what exactly happened.

A teacher, a Muslim man from Guyana, shot the girls disapproving looks when they re-enacted dance moves from Passa Passa videos. It wasn't a far stretch to imagine that same teacher not believing them if they came to him about sexual violence.

Why ya cack up ya batty fah?

We moved again, this time to a hotbed of Somaliniimo. The location was Weston Road and Lawrence Avenue West. The area had always been home to large populations of immigrants and had been the destination of people fleeing slavery down south. The neighbourhood had a Somali feel to it. Sunny afternoons brought out older men wearing sarongs and leaning on canes, chewing on *miswak*, a tooth cleaning plant. I didn't know what to make of it. Why the fuck were we moving so far from everything I knew?

I told my stepmother that when I graduated from university, I was leaving for good.

Go now then. What is stopping you?

Stupid bitch.

Our new building was a newer development. It sat at the foot of Hickory Tree Road. Beside it was Weston Lions Park, where soccer matches between immigrant men were played. They parked along the edge of the road and changed in front of their cars, showing the outlines of their penises. All week they suffered the indignities that came with low-wage work and now came the release of the referee's whistle. I enjoyed watching their matches. One of them, a squat Arab man, once asked if I wanted to play. I chuckled and said I was good. Bless his heart, he didn't know.

My last semester, I attended night school at a different school. I had failed Grade II math and without it I wouldn't receive my Ontario Secondary School Diploma. Without said diploma, entering a postsecondary institution was out of the question. I needed to get out of there, away from the constant misery and pain. So I took the bus each Tuesday and Thursday to Keele Street and Eglinton Avenue West, to York Memorial, an older school, replete with black-and-white photos of sports associations holding Gaelic and Welsh faces.

Monique was also taking a class and by the time we were there, the school was considerably less prestigious and less velum-coloured.

I began to plan my escape on the bus rides to Eglinton West station. I took detours with Monique so we could eat the barbeque chicken wings and fries we bought from the Chinese folks who ran the pizzeria across from the school. They had no seats and there was an old arcade game in the corner. As we glided past the Beth Israel *shul* and turned into the subway, we spat out the bones and licked the specks of barbeque sauce off the Styrofoam.

As night school wound down, I sat for the final exam. I ended up getting a failing grade yet again. The teacher, knowing I had applied for university, changed my 48 percent to 50 percent.

Monique was a young woman from the tiny island of Grenada. The summer I worked at the amusement park I found out she had a hole in her heart. It stopped her from going on any of the rides. I felt bad for her but she assured me that living was far more important to her than sitting on a roller coaster.

The boys at school were cruel to her and called her tar baby, darkie, night. Where did they get off commenting on her beautiful, creaseless, and luscious skin? She never broke out, yet they, with their slightly lighter faces, were covered in craters. Most of them, as it is with black men who hate themselves, dove deep into the pool of white girls with jungle fever. Oh well, not our loss. I had Monique and she made me feel like a winner. She told me not to back down and to fight.

I don't know what I would've done without these brilliant girls. I reflect on it as a grown man and my eyes fill with tears at their generosity. I will forevermore be grateful for the space they made in their lives, and hearts, for a boy who felt unwanted by the world.

Spirits boosted, I figured out what school I wanted to attend. We listened to hours of admissions staff from various universities and colleges expounding the virtues of their respective schools. I decided on Ryerson University early on and avoided people from other schools. Tamika decided that going to York was worth the danger of the empty spaces between the buildings and the frequency of sexual assaults on its campus. Monique considered the practical turn the economy was taking and wondered out loud if going to college, with a scholarship, was more conducive to the life she wanted than plodding through dry, theoretical bullshit. It was an exciting time for us all.

By June of 2003 I received an acceptance letter for Ryerson University's School of Urban and Regional Planning. Since I had spent less than four years at a Canadian school, I had been required to complete an English proficiency test. The other two schools that I had applied to charged several hundred dollars for it. Thankfully, Ryerson offered their own version at a third of the price. I spoke, wrote, and read English better than most white folks, but, hey, I took the damn test. It was no surprise when I received the acceptance letter but I was elated all the same.

Here I was, on my way away from the darkness of North York and Weston to the light, or so I thought, of a downtown university. What I was taught in the halls of my high school left me empowered and disillusioned with my adopted home. I skipped prom and graduation. I was happy with a signed yearbook and hugs from the girls who had my back.

Goodbye, my *bad gyals*, you never left my spirit.

GENTRIFICATION OF THE MIND

C.W. Jefferys was a cultural wasteland to me and departing for downtown seemed like an exit visa. I escaped the vast distances, the empty spaces, and the quiet suffering. I got away from the pervasive blackness. Before C.W. Jefferys, I hadn't attended a black majority school and when I arrived there, I couldn't wrap my head around no longer enjoying token status. In the Netherlands, I had crafted an identity that required being alien, distant, and exotic.

Ryerson could help me recapture that lost identity. I paraded around and wore my feigned exoticism like a peacock. I was delighted by white faces expressing shock, horror, and amazement at my experiences. I wanted to be unique and none of my West Indian friends gave me that. Time to get it from bougie white bitches instead.

The beginning of every school year at Ryerson was marked by something called Frosh Week. It helped new students become more familiar with each other, the staff, and the campus. I beheld white faces that couldn't stop smiling. Despite my desire, I was distressed at the thought of being the only black student in my class. Thankfully, I spotted another black face, and I went over to introduce myself.

Move from me. Battyboy.

I joined a game of duck, duck, goose. This type of corniness marked my entire career at this school. I got up and left. I couldn't take the forced happiness and constant smiling. I went to my part-time job to conduct market research with Canadians, coast to coast.

The campus was a mishmash of architectural styles. There was the social realism of the Depression and the Brutalism of the post-war period. Between these two horrid styles stood solitary Victorian and Edwardian buildings, usually housing student organizations.

The Urban Planning School was on the fourth floor of the Library Building. It was a hideous Brutalist building that made me feel inconsequential and small. Flyover walkways connected it to Kerr Hall, where most of our lectures took place. The school was named after Egerton Ryerson, the founder of the Ontario public school system. I didn't know this at the time, but he was an enthusiastic supporter of residential schools. In such schools, Indigenous children were sexually abused and stripped of their cultural heritage. This system claimed the lives of thousands of Indigenous children.

Away from the prying eyes of family, I transformed my exterior. Gone were the baggy clothes that drowned my bony frame. I wore tighter jeans, flowing shirts, and coats that weren't emblazoned with an American sports team.

The call centre I worked at gave us gift cards to the Eaton Centre, the giant mall near Ryerson. I took the $50 and $100 gift cards and headed straight for the sales racks of fancy stores. Not the type of fancy stores that line Toronto's ritzy Mink Mile, but the upscale versions of the garbage retailers that dotted suburban plazas.

I was determined not to let anything stop my transformation into a visible homosexual. I went so far as to utter that truth to one of my classmates. She was the granddaughter of Italian immigrants from Scarborough, an architectural abyss in the east of the city. She was the first person I came out to, but she wasn't fazed. I cut her off. I wanted her to be elated for me. I craved reassurance, and her indifference, albeit very tolerant, was intolerable to me.

I couldn't vibe with most of the other white students either. It wasn't for a lack of trying, but I didn't understand the suburban world many of them hailed from. They led lives that I watched on TV. They knew nothing of the ghetto beyond what they saw on TV.

So Mohamed, you're from Jane and Finch. Was it tough growing up there?

I smiled, as Canadians are wont to do, and explained how the intersection of zealous policing, poverty, underfunded schools, and overworked parents led to the social ills beamed into their living rooms.

I never hear anything good about the place. Was it difficult for you?

I grew tired of their anthropological intrigue. I took comfort in the fact that our professors called the suburbs of their youth *ill-conceived and perilous to the health of our environment*. If the ghetto created criminals, the suburbs created global warming.

The wonderful thing about Ryerson was that they had tons of books written by those of the Old and New Left. I browsed the stacks for hours and devoured any text by Lenin. He claimed the working class of Europe and North America had more in common with the descendants of freed slaves in the West Indies and the colonized of Africa than the middle classes or bourgeoisie of the West, who benefited the most from colonization. It gave me hope that in the future, I could shed my racialized existence and be at peace with everyone. Through revolution, we came closer together. We became *new people* by overthrowing *the yoke of imperialism*.

Eventually, I landed on Frantz Fanon. He helped me understand that I actually had more in common with my classmates from Jane and Finch than the people I now went to school with. In *Toward the African Revolution*, I read a line that hit me between the eyes:

The West Indian of 1945 is a Negro.

In my disavowing I forgot who I was in the white frame of reference. The truth was that *the Somali of 2003 was black.*

By gliding into the pools of my African-ness, I tapped into the flourishes of poets like Langston Hughes. He dreamt of Africa when he wrote:

> *I built my hut near the Congo and it lulled me to sleep.*
>
> *I looked upon the Nile and raised the pyramids above it.*

I quickly assembled a new group of friends. I maintained these friendships beyond my years at Ryerson. There was Ivy, the daughter of Grenadian immigrants and Majid, the son of Persian refugees. I got close with the daughter of Argentines who fled to Toronto because of the Dirty War. Her name was Venezia.

I met the last member of our crew, a young man named Roque, early on in the school year because he and I took the same bus to Lawrence West subway station. The thing that initially stopped us from getting on was our suspicion of each other. He told me, years later, that he thought I was giving him dirty looks. I chuckled because I thought the same thing of him. His parents had fled El Salvador in the late 1980s, as the American-sponsored slaughter of its people went into overdrive. His uncle, a fighter with the leftist Farabundo Martí National Liberation Front, had been injured by a bomb, and they fled to the Canadian embassy in San Salvador. There they were granted asylum. Years later this same uncle died in a car crash at Jane and Lawrence.

My first year of university is where I met a life-long partner of mine: alcohol. I was invited by two classmates to an all-you-can-eat Italian restaurant on the outskirts of the city. I made my way over from my call-centre gig and one of them asked if I wanted a drink. I requested pop, but she dismissed this.

Liquor, Mohamed.

I ordered a martini. I figured it had to be a decent drink since I saw starlets in movies ordering it. As the vermouth and gin concoction washed down my throat, I felt something I hadn't in years. This was how Valium made me feel. The anxiety I carried around all day was dulled by the properties of the liquor. Since I couldn't get doctors to give me Valium, I drank instead.

I took courses that introduced me to ideas about the city, its theories, its ways of controlling bodies— be they bodies of water or human bodies—and the spatial arrangement of Canadian cities.

We were taught the differences between inorganic and organic urbanization. What was the best form for the most amount of people? How could we, the future urban planners of Toronto, make the city a better place for majorities and minorities?

The whole thing spoke to me in ephemeral ways. I had applied to the school with the expectation that it was like the urban simulation games I played on the computer. Little did I know how much theory came with urban planning.

One of my favourite professors was a man from Trinidad and Tobago. We'll call him Professor

Johnson. He came to Canada in the 1970s to continue his studies at the University of Western Ontario in London. It was here that he was introduced to the pernicious form of Canadian racism. He told us about the time that he'd gone to a farmers' market in town. As he made his way past the stalls, he felt a wetness on his hand. He moved his hand forward, assuming it was the dew from the produce. As he continued walking, the wetness returned. He looked down and noticed a little white boy licking his hand. By the time the boy's mother noticed what was going on, our dear professor's eyes burned a hole into her. The little boy asked his mother why the black man didn't taste like chocolate. The mother turned red and apologized profusely. He shook his head and cautioned her against teaching her children ignorant shit.

It wasn't just his anecdotes that made his classes fun but the introduction of theories that would have taken a less enthusiastic pedagogue an entire semester to teach. His assignments were transformative. One of them took me from High Park loop to Main Street station, following the route of the 506 College streetcar. I retraced a walk he himself had taken a few years prior. With his text as a foundation for our assignment, I used his vision to see areas changed and buildings transformed.

Carlton Street had been sanitized of the homeless, and hipsters had driven out the Portuguese on Dundas Street West and the Italians on College Street. Urban displacement observed by a child of refugees. He begged us to consider spatiality and what that meant for someone who owned a home on Howard Park as opposed to a small business owner on Parliament Street. What did the man begging in Allen Gardens have in common with the working poor in the high-rises near Main Street and Danforth Avenue? He asked us to unearth the tensions of living in urban and productive spaces. Who got the spoils? Who set the agenda? Who was desirable?

A RAIN-BEARING
CLOUD AT NIGHT

Things at home weren't improving for me. I worked nearly forty hours a week and had a full course load. My stepmother's greed wore me down. She insisted I apply to any grant or bursary and hand over half of my paycheques.

Why weren't the other children working? I thought.

Isaac was fifteen and never applied for a job. Instead, he infected our family computer by downloading questionable files from questionable sites. He depleted our groceries and threw temper tantrums. Who was going to teach him how to use the washing machine or pay bills? Did you boil an egg for ten or five minutes? The only escape I had was the bottle. I drank more, but in the presence of fellow students, it didn't raise any eyebrows.

Ebyan, on the other hand, spent years in and out of the home and now she was getting married. She had found some lanky man who tolerated her bullshit. Her fiancé came saddled with a quarter-million dollars of debt, lack of stable employment, and a sense of aggrandizement inappropriate for a loser. He thought he was an artist because he was booked to play basement parties where he performed the classics of Somali music. The day before she was to get married, she told me she was going to the doctor. I threw her a quizzical glance.

Oh yeah, I'm getting the cutting opened up.

I took this in as she rambled on about what she was doing that day. I almost threw up in my mouth. I couldn't believe she never sought medical help! I forgot that she too was damaged by our experience. I hadn't had the room in my broken spirit to consider that, like me, she was a hostage to our outdated customs. Our stay in the West was marked by the surgical insistence of our ancient culture. I ran to the bathroom. I sat on the toilet and cried quietly. All my fear and loathing collided in that moment. If there was no hope for them, I wasn't going to fall victim to the jaws of our genes. I wasn't going to surrender to that which sought to undermine her and stone me.

Jane and Finch became an afterthought as I delved into urban abstractions and booze. I was becoming more confident about coming out so I told my old classmates at C.W. Jefferys the truth. I rang them and all but one received the news warmly. We won't dwell on the hater. She was a non-factor when I knew her. My girl Tamika was ecstatic. She had always been more advanced than the other students, but I was still nervous. In my deluded mind, I thought my need for dick wasn't legible in my mannerisms or behaviour.

Mo! I'm so happy you found your truth!

When we were at Jefferys, she yelled my name across the hall.

Are you going home, Mo!?

Everyone laughed and she apologized.

I just love calling you Mo. Maybe I'll stick with Mohamed going forward.

All was forgiven and we went back to being our *banjee* selves. My new friends at Ryerson, a pastiche of Canadian multicultural policy, feigned indifference or ran, in the case of the guys, toward humour to disguise their shock. They befriended someone who ate bootyholes.

Poor ghetto youth, free your mind!

I logged onto a gay chat room one afternoon in Kerr Hall and found a pretty Persian. I walked over to his place on Mutual Street, deep in the gay village. We watched some cheesy Persian film on his bulbous television, and he went about the business of climbing me. It felt like a finger was rapidly penetrating me. I made a face when he came and promptly got up to leave. I didn't expect my first sodomite experience to be this dull. He wanted to kiss me goodbye. I offered my hand.

Fuck you, you small-dicked bitch. These lips will swallow you whole!

The Internet was crucial to my cruising, or the act of finding dick. I went to a far-off computer lab and used any of the streetcar lines or subway stations that crisscrossed the campus to get to Sherbourne, Queen, Dundas, Bleecker, Wellesley, Bay, and so on. The men were white, and racialized flattery drew me in. I settled for them because the ones I desired didn't want me.

One was a muscle daddy with dentures. He lost his teeth to meth. He showed me what a proper blowjob was made off. I realized in my teenage years that swallowing was the business. I used to suck my own dick and hold on to the head as I came. It wasn't until this man did it on me that I realized it felt better when done by someone else.

Some of these queens offered me money, and I stopped seeing them. The assumption that I was a working queen was offensive. I may be a sad, deranged, masochistic, alcoholic bitch, but I had this sex for free. Fuck their money.

Another thing that kept popping up was condom use. Since I abstained from anal after my Persian experience, I didn't even get into it with them. Slowly, I noticed a few of them trying to penetrate me while I slept or was passed out from drinking.

I had to fight one guy after I found him on top of me in the morning. I don't know who the fuck he thought I was, but I'm not that bitch. No, ma'am.

My friends and I explored downtown neighbourhoods. The enormous size of Toronto was a gift from venerated premier Mike Harris. I wasn't afraid of going outside the core. Since most of them lived in opposite directions of me, I had to think long and hard about my return trip. Ivy lived in Malvern, Venezia in Mimico, Majid was near Parkway Forest Drive, and Roque lived just off Jane. Since Roque and I lived near each other, they came to us. Our first summer together was fun! Barbeques, picnics in parks, trips out to the countryside, and so on. We bonded and they learned from me.

What are you reading these days?

A thoughtful response was in order, since I was their smart friend.

Richard Wright, Zora Neale Hurston, Langston Hughes, Nella Larsen, and James Baldwin.

It was around this time I got into transgressive artists as well. J.G. Ballard was a favourite and Pasolini's films (but not his fiction, oddly) were a delight. Almodóvar's cinematic genius never ceased to amaze me. The one writer I owed more than any other was the Marquis de Sade. I took to de Sade like a fish to water. It was his total disregard of convention, morality, and decency that spoke to me. I checked out any book the library was allowed to stock. Sadly, *The 120 Days of Sodom* was not available when I went looking for it.

THE SPAN OF MY
UNCERTAIN YEARS

I t was a Saturday morning in 2004.

As we got ready for Quranic school, I heard a scream.

It was my stepmother, Samira.

She ran around the apartment pulling on her hair and beating her chest. I put my clothes on and quickly joined everyone in the living room.

As my stepmother explained, something terrible had happened to Ismahan.

Her sister's husband had molested the twelve-year-old light of my life. She was so young. Twelve years since we had welcomed our gift to Beatrix, Queen of the Netherlands.

My poor sister would never be the same again.

She was the only girl under our roof who'd been spared from genital cutting, but this . . . this seemed insurmountable.

I wanted to hold her and, at the same time, flee.

I felt useless.

Why, in *her* moment of need, was I consumed with how *I* was feeling?

Was I incapable of feeling for others?

Was my state of being the result of endless violence?

I got up to take a shower. I rested my head on the tiled walls, and the steam clouded my sight. My sobbing was drowned out by the falling water. The spray burned my skin.

Samira called her mother and sisters to a *shiir*, Somali for council.

There my delight was interrogated by the women of the family. My stepmother recounted some of these questions to us.

Did he hurt you?

How do you feel today?

Do you think you'll remember this when you get married?

Samira threatened to call the police.

My grandmother didn't take to that and thought airing the sordid affair shamed the family and harmed her granddaughter a great deal more than seeking justice.

These white people and their police don't care about little Somali girls.

Apparently, neither did the women in our family.

As the *shiir* concluded, my aunt's son, the spawn of the predator, attacked my stepmother. But he was on the ground before he knew what happened. Samira began shouting at him.

Warya, I used to take bitches out to the desert and slaughter them. Ask your worthless mother.

She left with her sunken soul and forlorn daughter.

Had she ever made the connection between her violence against me and the crippling assault against her flesh and blood? Had she considered the damage done to me as I woke to her furious fists? Did she think she was as evil as the man who helped himself to her daughter's body? Did she think about how she violated my trust in my elders?

The truth was she didn't care about my bodily dignity. What I felt inside didn't matter because I hadn't escaped her body, modified in the name of our Lord.

I spent that week taking hot showers. My skin felt raw. I wasn't going to stand for this anymore. After that day, I was done. I was leaving.

Fuck them.

In May of 2005, I spiralled out of control. It was a balmy Sunday and I was nursing a hangover. The girls were gone for the weekend, leaving me alone with Samira and Isaac. She was having a bad day and took out all the dishes, utensils, pots, and pans. I was to clean them and the kitchen. After I finished, I had to make dinner. Isaac sat in front of the TV playing video games. I am unsure of what triggered her, but as I stood on a stool to reach the dusty shelves, my stepmother yanked me down and pummelled me.

I snapped. I pushed her to the ground.

You're not my mother! I hate you!

I ran out and sat in the stairwell. I cried quietly as I heard them calling out for me. I was going to kill myself. I didn't finish cleaning. I went straight to my bedroom and reached for my bag.

There were two bottles of pills. I went into the bathroom and noticed a bottle with Fadumo's name on it. She had been in a car accident and had been prescribed pain medication. I downed them all. I called the friends I made at Ryerson to say goodbye. One was out of the country. One was playing a basketball game and couldn't talk. Another was already in bed, getting rest for the next day's work. The last one was in the middle of a field out in the country and the rates were going to kill him. I drifted into a sleep and hoped not to greet the morning.

The following was recounted to me years later by my younger brother: I got up in the middle of the night and collapsed in the hallway, in a pool of my own urine. He alerted my stepmother, who decided to change me out of my soiled pants and clean up before calling 9-1-1.

I awoke at the old Keele site of the Humber River Hospital, yelling that Samira drove me to this. She didn't come into the hospital room. She told Fadumo she felt guilty.

I was in the hospital for about two weeks. One of the other patients was a short white man who called law offices and threatened to sue his former business partner. The nurses told me that he had a nervous breakdown when his mother died. He never owned a business.

There was a young black woman who comforted the other patients. For the entirety of the first day, I thought she was a nurse. When I saw her being led to a room, I figured it out. Then there was the young black man I made eyes with. He got into it with an orderly and a fight ensued. He was sedated and strapped to his bed. I looked through the glass and blew him kisses. I wish I could've saved him.

In *The Trap: What Happened to Our Dream of Freedom*, Adam Curtis analyzes the rise of the anti-psychiatry movement, and specifically R.D. Laing.

In the documentary, he mentions an experiment by a group of young psychiatrists who committed themselves. They wanted to prove that the profession was predicated on a power imbalance, allowing for all sorts of abuses. I learned that by agreeing with the doctor and whatever assessment he cooked up, I would get discharged sooner. Ten days after trying to take my own life, I was back home. I acquiesced to power, until I could escape it.

I was told that for the sake of my nerves I would be taking an extended vacation to the Middle East and Somalia. I was happy to get away from home and my ruined scholastic life. Before touching down in the lands of the East, I planned a pit-stop in the capital of the Empire, London.

Before going on vacation, my stepsister Fadumo had asked me to accompany her to First Canadian Place, a downtown office tower in Toronto, to meet with lawyers for an insurance company. It was to finalize the terms of a settlement for the car accident. The collision had been caused by a speeding motorcyclist. He had rear-ended her boyfriend's car. The guy on the bike died but the police, after talking to witnesses, concluded he was at fault. On our way to Lawrence West station, she told me she heard my delirious ravings in the hospital.

I know all about your sick life. How much you love dick and how much you hate us. You need to come clean to hoyo, because she's been blaming herself. It's not fair she's beating herself up when you're the sick one.

I always felt close to Fadumo. Samira mocked her awkwardness, quiet disposition, her size, and lopsided smile. She watched gay men on television and commented on how amazing they were.

I wish I had a gay friend!

I wanted her to know that I was fiercer than those queens. What she meant was that homosexuality in white bodies was acceptable. As a Somali, I disgraced our heritage. Queerness was a fine complement to the Western degeneracy we inhabited, yet in our Islamic culture, it was a symptom of sickness. Why on Earth would she want sickness for her brother!

I'm doing this because I love you.

I told Samira my truth and the relief was legible in her demonic face.

I knew it wasn't me! Go and pray away that filth!

She decided that upon my arrival I was to be hitched to some woman in Somalia. I packed a suitcase and one of her friends drove me to the airport. As we glided across the multi-storey highway, one of them asked if I was feeling all right.

We heard you were in the hospital.

I smiled and nodded. She heard I went into diabetic shock. I smiled.

Sugar is a big problem for me.

I checked in and waited for my flight. I was six hours early.

On the plane, I sat next to two Chinese women who had been born in Malaysia but raised in Toronto's Chinatown. They were part of that wave of immigration that followed the senior Trudeau's reforms. After spending their lives working, they purchased a lovely home in Markham, yet another architectural abyss in the suburbs, and now spent their retirement travelling. They fed me shots of liquor and we played cards. Apparently, they were only transiting in London. Their final destination was a Mediterranean cruise. They warmed my heart. My favourite story of theirs involved one of them buying a live chicken on Spadina Avenue. They don't sell live animals in today's Chinatown. Future Chinatown probably won't have Chinese people, if those in Toronto who gentrify have anything to do with it.

At Gatwick airport, I was met by a brother of my father's. He was the progeny of some woman my grandfather married after ditching my paternal grandmother. He was a squat man who couldn't shut up to save his life. He pointed out every landmark we passed on the train to Victoria station. I looked out onto the terraced backyards and wondered what sort of lives the polite, middling classes of suburban London led.

Somewhere in that mix was the sage of Shepperton, James Graham Ballard. The flyovers of the M23 brought to life the words in *Concrete Island*, *The Atrocity Exhibition*, and *Crash*.

The landscape of London was more eye-catching than the cityscape I had left behind. I marvelled at the Georgian and Victorian buildings, which seemed in harmony with the Brutalist and postmodernist forms that pockmarked this regal city. It took awhile to figure out how to cross the street, and when locals found out I was not American, they lost all interest. Americans are so much cooler than Canadians.

After transferring onto the underground at Victoria station, we made our way further north to Burnt Oak station. It was in the fourth zone and populated by working-class Englishmen, Nigerians, Turks, Somalis, and South Asians. Burnt Oak Broadway, the main drag, held ethnic grocery stores, gambling parlours, and off-licences, a sort of convenience store that carried liquor. I was introduced to my uncle's family, which consisted of three girls and a boy. His wife was a lovely woman who didn't know how to cook. I was given a small room upstairs and spent the rest of the day sleeping. My hay fever was in overdrive, and in the morning I awoke to find my eyelids sealed shut by dried pus.

My uncle took me around town. He invited his cousin, who once drove a tour bus. We visited palace after palace. Piccadilly Circus I could do without, but I was interested in the area around his office. He had a contract with the Home Office that saw him acting as a liaison between the state and the Somali community of west London. We took the train along the Bakerloo line, and as we exited at Queen's Park, I marvelled at the various faces and tongues, fashions and hairstyles.

The place felt more alive than Toronto, even if the people didn't smile as much. I saw myself living here. I visited my stepmother's relatives in the east end of the city. Around Finsbury, Islington, and Highbury, I found pockets of beautiful people doing hip things such as queer hip hop and new takes on gender-bending. Seven Sisters Road was home to sexy Cypriots, none of whom climbed my bony back.

On one of his tours, my uncle confided in me about a salacious secret. Before reuniting with his wife in London, he had spent a few years alone. To keep his loneliness at bay, he took another wife. A few more years passed and the first wife was set to arrive. Not knowing what to do, he came clean. The first wife was not having it and he quietly divorced the second wife. He had a child with the second wife. The little girl was the cutest thing!

Normally, she avoids strangers.

I smiled and kept making goofy faces, much to her delight.

I was told by another relative, part of the caravan calling on me, to visit the British Museum. I jotted it down and planned a trip for the weekend. When I asked about the cost, they looked at me inquiringly.

Warya, museums in this country are free.

I wish that legacy had been passed on to Toronto's Anglos, who charged for museums. As I entered the rotunda, I stood beneath a glass ceiling. The summer's light gave a fairytale quality to the Greco-Roman facade inside the building. It was a weaving together of ancient Europe, imperial Britain, and postmodern London. I was excited. I took in the Elgin Marbles, the Benin Bronzes, and other loot from their heyday as an empire. In the basement, I found African statues made of wood and totem poles from West Coast Indigenous nations. As per usual, we were relegated to the basement of history.

Meanwhile, the second Gulf War with the second Bush didn't seem to die down. Bush Jr. had, rather prematurely, declared victory. His ally in the destruction of Iraq was the MP for Sedgefield, County Durham. Most of us know him as Prime Minister Tony Blair. Blair had an urge to wage war, but unlike Eden or Thatcher, he masked it with a do-gooder veneer that placated the humanitarians in his party.

I remember when Blair premiered this schtick. He was going to save the victims of the Serbian genocides but, in doing so, wanted to rewrite the mission of British liberal democracy in a world devoid of the Soviet spectre. When he was bombing Serbians, not many Muslims objected. As America's foremost ally, Britain signed on early to unseat Saddam Hussein and his clan of psychopaths.

As the centre of the Levant devolved into suicide bombings, kidnappings, beheadings, and a return to medieval Islam, Blair & Co. was unwilling to admit its mistake.

There was rage bubbling beneath the surface. Young men of my faith felt alienated and emasculated by liberal democracy. They were asked to consider Jews and gays to be their fellow citizens and respect their right to be. They were told that women had rights and no belief system was superior to another. The police viewed them suspiciously for the way they dressed and practised their faith. On television, their holy Prophet was being called a pedophile. These young men watched Internet videos of

Muslim mothers weeping as American bombs dispatched their kin. Whole villages in Muslim lands were wiped out by the Christian's bellicosity and it was served up as news.

They were told they were British but they were treated like a fifth column by the tabloid press. Documentaries purported to show how bad Muslim girls had it locally and globally. These young men felt the need to strike back using the only weapon they could wield with total and nihilistic certainty. Their loyalty was to the *umma*, not the queen.

On July 7, 2005, I woke to a BBC announcer's lamentations. As he took calls, I pulled the plug. My nose was congested and their accents on the radio made the hangover torturous. I closed my eyes and thought about the statuesque man I had spent the night dancing with. His skimpy outfit barely contained his bubble butt. It popped out from underneath the stretchy mesh of his bottoms. I squeezed it softly and he smiled. At some point, he held up a baggy of white powder and we were off. He poured some out on his erect penis and after sniffing it, I went to town on it.

A few hours after my debauchery came to an end, a group of disgruntled youth from Luton boarded trains bound for London. In their backpacks they carried bombs.

I heard my uncle yelling. I lugged my body downstairs and put on the kettle.

Mohamed! Thank God you're here. There's been a terrorist attack on the underground.

I looked at him and continued making tea. What did he expect of me? I didn't care who died. I needed all of life for myself. I went outside for a smoke and noticed our Turkish neighbour yelling. Apparently, some hooligan had set his car on fire. Such fine people!

As the hysteria over the bombings subsided, my father decided I should come to the Middle East at the end of July. I didn't want to marry anyone, let alone someone in a country I hadn't been to since I was four. My father was a loathsome man. As a boy in the Netherlands, seeing my friends with their fathers always filled me with fury. I wasn't sure if I was upset at their joy or angry with the man who created me.

Television showed me what I was missing. Fathers going to sports games with their sons or rescuing them from evildoers. I watched a commercial for razors showing a young boy imitating his father as he shaved.

Save for the material support, it didn't feel like I had a father. There were no pictures of the two of us that allowed me to access some memory of him.

Whenever he did call, he gave me the usual spiel about staying out of trouble and doing well in school.

My dream for you is to become a doctor and make us all proud.

How did he expect this happen without any encouragement? At home I was degraded, and at school I was made to feel bad about my mannerisms and my discoloured teeth. It was a miracle that I didn't fall victim to some child molester. I was ripe for the picking.

Looking back, those were lonely years. The only escapes I had were the television shows beamed in from America. It was the travails of characters in books that helped me cope with my own struggles. My father's absence was excused by my stepmother.

You are so ungrateful. Would you like him to live here with us so we can be poor?

What was wrong with being poor and happy? I got the sneakers I wanted and I played soccer, but I was the kid whose parents didn't show up.

To absolve him from any responsibility, I told myself there was no way he knew about the violence. I dreamt about him rescuing me from this hell, but life eventually showed me otherwise.

Years later, when we had relocated to Toronto, he paid us a visit. We had a conversation in Weston Lions Park, just behind our building. He looked me in the face and told me he knew what my stepmother had been doing to me.

He was the only person I had a smidgen of faith in, but now I wanted to pummel him.

His logic was that my life was infinitely better with my stepmother in the West than with my biological mother back in Somalia.

The only thing I ever wanted was his love and affection. All he seemed to want for me was to have what he didn't: material comfort.

As we made our way back into the building he asked me if we were good. I smiled and kept walking.

Fuck you, daddy dearest.

RUN, MOHAMED, RUN

rang Ivy, my Grenadian friend from Ryerson, and told her to get me a ticket back to Toronto. I didn't consider returning to the Netherlands because that Mohamed no longer existed. The future Mohamed was in Toronto. When she called me back, everything was sorted. I took some of the money my father had sent me and wired it to her, using a service that sent money anywhere in the world in twenty-four hours or less. I was due to fly out on July 17, 2005.

My father began calling daily. He usually called once or twice a week. I had been in London for almost six weeks at that point, and my uncle, frustrated that I was constantly out, decided to tell me the secret himself. Apparently, my father had taken another wife.

Wait, that's not all of it.

He produced two children with this woman. One of them was already a toddler, meaning this union wasn't brand-new.

I was shocked. I thought my father couldn't sink any lower but here we were. I took a drag from my cigarette and looked at my uncle. Fuck this. Fuck him. Fuck you.

Is that it? I'm tired and want to sleep.

Meanwhile, back in Toronto, my stepmother had to find out by opening the mail.

Apparently, my father had sent her a letter informing her that he divorced her. The way he did this was by going to the mosque and in front of an imam proclaimed it three times:

In the name of Allah, I divorce you.

The question now was how to divide their property in Somalia. For years, my father had been busily constructing a hospital and a hotel, on land he had bought on the shoreline in the city of Bosaso, in northern Somalia. He wasn't keen on letting my stepmother have her rightful half.

I mean, what did she expect from my father? Did she think he had a moral compass?

Before I departed London, I wanted to visit Yusuf and his family. The same year we left for Toronto, they moved across the North Sea to Great Britain.

They had settled in Leicester before moving to White City in west London. It was there I called on Iron Eyes. She welcomed me in.

You should've told me you were coming today. I would have cooked you something!

I made due with tea, *halwa,* and samosas and asked her about her sons. Her head dropped.

Your friend is a lost cause. He started selling drugs when we lived in Leicester. I thought by moving away, I saved him. Meanwhile, his younger brother got into this gangster garbage too!

She smacked her chest.

My heart, I found a gun under his pillow. That was it. I told him to go, and I sent Daud to study the Quran in Yemen.

Apparently, while he was in Yemen, he studied with a Sufi mystic and now was a vegetarian.

Yusuf got worse. He started smoking that crack. He hangs out by Wembley with some black girl. This is all her fault. He never smoked that shit before he met her.

I kissed her goodbye. I made my way to Wembley Stadium, but I couldn't find my beloved. Perhaps it was for the best. I remember when his brother told him their father had died, Yusuf didn't cry. He later told me he didn't want me to see him cry. His job was to protect me. I hope he found peace.

I will always love him.

★ ★ ★

I was on track for my escape, and no marital bullshit was going to stand in my way.

I went to Finsbury Park to see Ismahan and Isaac, who'd arrived from Toronto. They told me their mother was flying out later that week. My father forbade me from seeing her. They were in London supposedly to visit me, but I knew Samira was plotting something. Perhaps she was using them to stall my departure for the Middle East. She knew how to hold people hostage.

I bade them farewell, knowing I might never again see them.

Ismahan was more outwardly religious after the abuse. I worried she'd turn into the equivalent of a nun and not allow love from a man or woman to enter her life. I worried the trauma was going to render her a victim, but . . . she was not that. I wanted her to survive and thrive, but as I held her bony frame, I knew I'd never see her achieve wondrous things. This was going to be my journey into the desert.

When the morning of the 17th came, I quietly walked down the stairs and put my suitcase outside. I grabbed my backpack and forgot to turn the computer off.

After my unannounced departure for Toronto, my uncle reported me missing to the London police. When the cops turned up at his home, he told them I spent hours on the computer. When one of them sat down to see what I was looking at, some gay porn flashed across the screen. I was told later he didn't know how to turn off the moaning of a giant black man being penetrated by another.

Unaware of all this, I ran with my suitcase to the Burnt Oak tube station and I remember passing an Arab vomiting outside of a betting shop. I felt so free. The wind felt new.

At Gatwick airport, I felt secure enough to sit down and let out a deep sigh. This relief was dispelled by a man in a suit. He approached me as I stood in line for a boarding pass.

I could fast-track you, sir. If you don't mind stepping over here, please.

I smiled and pretended not to hear him.

If you cooperate sir, this will go a lot smoother.

He read the confusion in my face.

You've been selected randomly for a security check. Could I see your passport?

I handed it over and felt the eyes of fellow passengers on me.

Why was I being treated with such suspicion? Did these assholes not know the personal risk I took to get to this blasted airport! I didn't have time for security theatre. I wanted to be free.

As if it couldn't get worse, I misread the gate number. As I got to Gate 205, I saw Haredi Jewish men and women in the waiting area. I looked out on the tarmac and saw a jetliner emblazoned with the blue and white of the Israeli flag. I made my way back to the screens with the gate information and a man in overalls, covered in oil stains, approached me. He demanded to see my passport. I wondered why a technician in an airport wanted to see my passport. I complied and figured he was some Mossad bastard.

You are in the wrong terminal.

In the end, I got on the right flight to Toronto. The plane ran out of gas, and we stopped in Montreal to refuel.

Arriving in my hometown, I was singled out, again, by immigration officials.

I was placed in a windowless room at Pearson. I sat there for four hours until officials concluded I wasn't a security risk.

Canada, and the other white societies of the West, want us immigrants to be loyal and willing to die for their democracies yet see no hypocrisy in treating us as suspects.

Before I got back, I had made arrangements with my old friend Tamika. She had told me I could stay with her family in Brampton, a suburb west of Toronto. I met her at a mall adjacent to the airport. There, she gave me three hundred dollars and bad news.

You see, Mo, my dad is an asshole. He thinks that you'll touch my little brother.

Her little brother wasn't quite two years old then.

I hope the money helps.

I put my fairy ass back on the bus. Then I broke down on the ride to Islington station.

That night I slept in the rain.

While I was in London, I had started writing short stories. It began as a way to stave off boredom. Everything I carried was soaked, and the stories I wrote in the United Kingdom were ruined.

One of them had been about a mortician who infected his wife. The illness, which could only be contracted from corpses, rendered her infertile. When she found out he had been fucking dead bitches, she chopped him into small bits and fed him to her dogs.

The story wasn't that good, so I never rewrote it.

When the rain stopped, I took my suitcase and walked past the bars of Queen Street West, hoping to catch a familiar face. That night, I saw no one and I doubt anyone saw me.

As the week progressed, I figured out what to do. I spent my nights at a youth hostel located near the corner of King Street West and Spadina Avenue. I doubt it's still there, considering how much gentrification ruined that street.

Venezia's mother referred me to a men's shelter near the bus terminal on Bay Street. When I got there, the woman at the front desk said I was too young for their shelter. She made a few calls. A youth shelter in Scarborough had a bed for me. It was called Second Base.

As I made my way from Kennedy station, past a mosque and Sri Lankan restaurants, I saw my new home. It was in the back of a parking lot, beside an Anglican church.

I spent the first weekend rooming with a white gay man, who was ejected by the time Sunday rolled around. He was replaced by a tall Ugandan man. We bonded over our fathers' marital choices. His stepmother was a witch, and he recounted the ways she tortured him.

I was broke and in need of work. I found a gig with an Australian company specializing in prospectuses. A prospectus is a document showing the progress of an investment fund, including several motions. My job was to call those people who hadn't voted and convince them to do so along with the board. Of course, this was before the boards, syndicates, and governments of the Earth plunged the global economy into the financial crisis of 2008.

I made little effort to explain to the holders of the funds what they were voting on. I felt vindictive. If they were going to be ignorant about their own money, oh well. My job wasn't to look out for their interests. This society, underwritten by crooked finance and usury, didn't look after my interests. Now I was bathing in the same waste it sprayed me with.

By December of that year, I settled into my new life. Through the Toronto Community Housing Corporation, the youth shelter got me a one-bedroom apartment in a government project called Gordonridge. It was about ten minutes, by bus, to Warden station. It had grocery stores, banks, and liquor stores nearby.

I made the mistake of accepting a mattress from the youth shelter. Back then, very little was known about the burgeoning bedbug problem. I had the fucking things in my apartment for years. I used to go to the office to book an exterminator, but they returned within weeks. I went through countless couches, dining tables, computers, televisions, books, and quilts.

I took to sleeping in the bathtub with socks over my hands. Even there, they found me. I found out that bedbugs had heat receptors that allowed them to seek out prey by their body heat. My apartment was on the fifteenth floor and the balcony was useless. Pigeons made their home in every nook and cranny and I smoked my cigarettes in the threshold of the door. I did most of my drinking outside so my boozing didn't feel like a problem.

I used to receive a GST refund cheque every three months. Since my sources of income varied, I relied on all of them equally. When one cheque was late, I was quick to call the agency dispensing them. I got on the phone with Revenue Canada and informed them that I didn't get my sixty-dollar cheque. According to the voice on the other end, a cheque had been mailed out. I asked what address they sent it to. It had gone to my stepmother's. I was asked to sign an affidavit that said I didn't receive or cash the cheque.

After returning the affidavit, I was sent a picture of a young man at a bank machine. I strained to make out who it was, but once I got my glasses on, I saw it was my brother Isaac. Enclosed in the envelope was the signed cheque and it wasn't my signature.

I couldn't believe his mother and sisters got him to commit a federal crime! It was astounding that their greed knew no limits. I called to give them the heads-up about a potential investigation into their crime.

My prospectus flogging job ended when my Australian employer moved their operations down south. Perhaps to be closer to their victims?

I then landed myself a summer-student position with the city's accessible bus service, Wheel-Trans. It was located near the lake, in the east end of Toronto.

One customer used to ask for me and kept me on the phone forever! She was over seven feet tall and had issues lugging her giant body around, hence her reliance on the service. She said she was in love with me. After returning from a day off, I was told by another student that she had visited the office. She wouldn't leave until she saw me. The staff took her on a tour of the office to show her I wasn't there.

By the end of that year, I landed a sweet gig with another transit agency. This one was with the commuter service that ran between Hamilton, Oshawa, Kitchener, Richmond Hill, Milton, Stouffville, and Union in Toronto. My first job was in their call centre, dispensing scheduling information to travellers. Then I moved up to transit control. The cracking voices of conductors who hit someone will never leave me. Some of these were suicides, which we were able to see on CCTV. Whatever happened to killing yourself at home?

By 2006, after three years at Ryerson, I was kicked out because I had failed statistics for the second time. I couldn't handle the full course load and a full-time job.

My friends, with their tuitions and board taken care of, thought I wasn't pushing myself hard enough. Did they think I was some magical negro in a Hollywood flick?

I was a young man who was trying to survive in a world that didn't want me. The fact that they couldn't see this came to fracture every one of my friendships with them. What did they know about having a parent beat you every single day since you were a child? What did they know about having said parent defraud you? What did they know about coming out? What did they know about being sent abroad to be wed to some stranger?

The truth is that they didn't, and they made very little effort to find out. Instead, they complained about my complaining. It was as though I ought to be grateful for merely existing. The concerns of a black queen don't matter if you silence him.

Despite that, the friends I made at Ryerson had a huge impact on my life. They moved me into my first apartment, took me out for dinners and—in the case of one and her family—housed me. I thought these relationships were made permanent by their knowledge of my personal tragedies. Little did I consider how important productivity and money were to them. I can't fault them for conforming to the Protestant work ethic that permeates "caker" culture.

When Italians began arriving in Toronto, they were shocked by the amount of cake and pastries their Anglo and Irish co-workers ate. They began calling them *mangia cake*, or cake eaters. Today, the moniker has been shortened to caker and is a catch-all term for uncouth or uncultured white folks who follow hockey, put mayo on everything, and regard men like Rob Ford as heroes.

When Venezia's mother offered me the apartment on the side of their house, I was elated. I was tired of living with bedbugs. I didn't consider that the reason she asked me was because I had been working for the province for a while and had passed my probationary period. The bedbugs were a cover. What she was after was a tenant who would forgo a lease. This came back to haunt me years later as I slid into my second stint of homelessness.

The part that stung was that I felt like I was part of their family. They invited me to every Jewish and Christian holiday while I lived there. Every single one of their birthdays. I was present for countless barbeques. Perhaps they saw me that way too, but I didn't walk away feeling like family.

I felt used.

In the spring of 2007, I was on my way to Calabogie, a town of four corners between Ottawa and Toronto.

One thing I enjoyed about Canada was the vast expanses of pristine nature. I was accustomed to the imitative nature of Dutch wildlife, all of it sculpted by man. When the Dutch camp, they mean a trailer in a field, adjacent to a waterpark or a nudist colony.

On the Calabogie trip, my companion Roque rented a cottage with an outdoor shower, but the temperature was in the single digits, so it was of little use. As we made our way down the 401, then up Highway 15, we made a pit-stop in Bancroft for supplies.

You guys must be from the city!

I smiled at the cashier and said I'd pay with debit.

After I made everyone dinner, I checked my voicemail.

Mohamed, this is Fadumo. I was hoping to tell you this instead of leaving a message, but your mom is here. She's staying at a hotel near the airport, but she won't be here for long. Hopefully you answer the next time we call.

What was she doing with them? She had moved to the Minneapolis–Saint Paul area after her sister sponsored her. I went back downstairs and played drinking games with everyone.

Everything all right, Mo?

I smiled at Roque and raised my shot glass.

I'm not sure when I stopped thinking about my mother. I wondered what she'd make of her adult son. Would she disapprove of my alcoholism? Disown me for my sexuality? Did she think my life was best served remaining a Muslim? It wasn't a good time to peddle maternal feelings to me. The boy she remembered died a thousand deaths and from his ashes rose up an icy queen. Fadumo called back the next day and put her on the line.

Mohamed, this is your mother. I have been waiting to hear your voice for so long. We drove up here just to see you, but your sister says you are out of town? Do you think you could come back to see us?

My friend had driven us here to Calabogie, and I wasn't going to interrupt the party. So, my mother returned to Minnesota without seeing me.

My stepmother didn't tell me this then, but apparently she told my real mother I worked as a hooker for rich old white men.

My mother kept calling over the years, but I found excuses not to see her or talk.

I began ignoring her calls.

Then I received an email from my father informing me that my birth mother was gravely ill and he pleaded with me to go see her. I deleted it without responding.

Apparently, she had gone to the emergency room for a pain in her side. After conducting tests, doctors found cancerous tumours all over her body and placed her in a hospice.

She died not long after.

I'm not sure where she's buried.

She was gone, for good now.

Any chance of reuniting was dashed by my indifference.

When friends asked me how I was feeling, I shrugged.

Perhaps, I was more like my father than I'd cared to admit.

THERE WERE NIGHTS THAT CAN NEVER BE FORGOTTEN

Eating had been a way for me to exercise control over my life. My stepmother caught on early and took delight in using food as punishment. *Off to bed. No dinner for you.*

I turned the punishment on its head and combined food denial with vomiting. I was excited when I gagged on some foreign taste, giving me the chance to sequester myself in the bathroom, the only place I was free in my despicable behaviour.

During the month of Ramadan, we starved ourselves out of some deluded sense of obligation to a faith that casts us as underlings in a modern world. Once, a classmate asked me if I felt a sense of spiritual enrichment.

No, I'm just hungry.

In hindsight, I wasn't the only one with a problematic relationship with food in my family. Isaac seemed to have the opposite problem. Instead of denying himself anything, he scarfed down seconds and thirds. When he was younger, Samira saw no problem with this and encouraged him to eat. I made fun of his ballooning weight and asked him if he remembered wearing dresses as a little boy. He cried and through his tears accused me of lying.

I'm not lying. Go ask hoyo.

She broke it to him gently and his crying grew more audible. Years later, I received a call from him. He said he was calling to tell me grandma had died. I answered calls from my family and engaged them in superficial conversations. I did it to show them I wasn't afraid of them. Their voices no longer had the power to induce anxiety. My brother, on the other hand, wanted an ear. He had told me about his life and how it had spiralled out of control. He stopped speaking to friends and couldn't keep amorous relationships together. I lit a cigarette and sat on the steps outside.

All I see is you laying on the floor. I can't shake it.

I wanted to cry.

I don't blame you for that, but I just want you to say sorry.

I couldn't take it anymore and turned the phone off.

I sat there, for all my neighbours to see, and cried. I didn't know what to make of such a demand. I was in bed for a week and refused to see anyone.

Nothing, it seemed, shook my sense of guilt.

I hated to think that at the root of his dishevelled life was my cry for help. Looking back, he was a silent ally of mine. When his mother asked him about my deviancy, he stated it was none of his business. She pounced on him and struck him twice across the face.

I wanted him to escape but where would he go? He was a mama's boy and never grew out of it. All he wanted from me was an acknowledgement that I had failed as his older brother. He didn't demand a pound of flesh, but I couldn't do it. I was proud of what I had done, and here he was asking me to revise my own hagiography. I never told him I was sorry.

The shock of my brother's distress and my grandmother's passing drove me to drink.

I had seen less and less of my grandmother after Ismahan's molestation.

She had left Canada to live with one of her sons in Harringay, a borough in northeast London.

The space between Somalia's wreckage and the nightmare of diaspora collided in the body of my grandmother. When she was fifteen her mother died suddenly. Her father remarried but her stepmother didn't care to take on the responsibility of raising another woman's children, a running theme among Somali families. She worked for an Italian family in Mogadishu. At the time, Italians were the colonial masters in our land and treated us as inferiors, both culturally and racially.

By her old age, she had moved from Somalia to Sweden to Canada. Her purse was full of spearmint candy and she wore shoes with Velcro straps. She told me about her days as a young woman and bemoaned that my stepsisters didn't engage the world beyond parties or weddings.

I didn't know she was illiterate until I accompanied her to the bank one day. When she was asked to endorse a cheque, she signed with an X. I went home and consulted the Internet about this. I didn't understand the value of literacy until that day.

Borges, in his infinite wisdom, extolled the act of reading as much as the act of writing.

My grandmother, like Borges, loved it when people read to her, albeit it was the Quran and not works of Occidental fiction. Years later, she left Canada for London's Finsbury neighbourhood. She lived down the street from that neighbourhood's infamous mosque.

Eventually, she died of a stroke. She endured the surging pain for two days because her children assumed she was sleeping. I had no way of making sense of her death until I remembered what a teacher at C.W. Jefferys had told us. In high school I had attended Friday prayers led by a chemistry teacher from Guyana. He conducted a short sermon wherein he told us that the position we died in was an indication of the life we led.

She died helplessly in her own waste, writhing with pain, unable to call out for help.

May Allah have mercy on her soul.

THE MORASS OF VICE
AND LIBERTINAGE

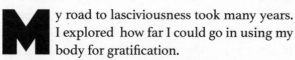y road to lasciviousness took many years. I explored how far I could go in using my body for gratification.

But what a distance one must first have ventured along the road of vice to arrive at that point!

Those words were spoken by a character in de Sade's *120 Days of Sodom*.

I scoped out magazines at the top of the rack in stores. I skipped past the curtain in video stores and beheld covers showing women covered in semen or multiple dicks sitting on a smiling face.

I used household items to see how much I could take. I used a glass deodorant bottle to probe my asshole. I thought about whether I should lube up the staircase railing and slide back onto it. I wanted to know how much pain my dick could take. I had a particular pen I used. I slid the hard plastic frame into my urethra and felt it expand.

My greatest feat was when I got the showerhead inside of me. When I yanked it out, blood ran down my leg.

Perhaps that is why someone like de Sade excites and fascinates me. He is willing to commit his body, spirit, and mind to the pleasures borne out by the body and conjured up by the mind.

I gawked at every bulge in school and imagined how much it could take before it was covered in my bloodied shit. My thoughts involved teachers, neighbours, my own father, friends, and Quranic instructors. I was in possession of the language needed for the acts.

The men who reached out to me insisted I dominate them. There was something within white gay culture that inscribed onto the black form a sexual aggression. I lacked that aggression, so I became a curiosity.

Why won't you force your black dick down my throat?

I didn't know how to answer this.

Interracial porn insisted I was active and my partner submissive. My whole life, submission had been stressed. I lowered my eyes when speaking to elders because the faith demanded it. I used to pray five times a day in the direction of Mecca because that was what my bondage to Allah required. That demand for submission was now flipped on its head. All I wanted was a throbbing dick inside of me and to submit to its uncut charms.

There were moments in my journey that were essential. The type of sex I engaged in over the years disgusted my gay friends, to say nothing of the corny, straight ones. The first eye-opening encounter lasted all of twenty minutes. I was working in a computer lab at school, pulling an all-nighter. Back then, before geotagging hookup apps, I had to contend with gay.com.

The photos, when a profile had one, were blurry.

I went out on a limb and decided to meet this guy. He told me to hop into a taxi as it was already close to 3 a.m. I went from Yonge Street and Dundas Street West to Bedford Road and Dupont Street. He met me downstairs. The Muslim cabbie, a bearded man from Afghanistan, looked at me quizzically as the older, bald, muscular man walked toward the driver's window.

This is who you are meeting?
I nodded.
But he is a gay!

I nodded. I kissed the stranger to mess with the driver. We got upstairs and he blew me on the glass steps leading to the second floor. I was in heaven. He kept my dick in his mouth long after I came, and the darkness made it difficult to see where one step ended and the other started.

I have to piss.

He kept the damn thing in his mouth.

Just do it in my mouth.

I pissed, and it was great!

His eyes bulged, and he tried to keep up with the flow of ammonia. I didn't know this, but more seasoned watersports enthusiasts released streams gradually. I treated his mouth like a urinal.

Not a drop spilled, because as I left his apartment and descended the staircase, I felt nothing on the soles of my feet.

I reached the height of my Sadean endeavours in a basement on Broadview Avenue, just south of Queen Street East. I was there at the behest of an older black man who wanted to run his tongue over my throbbing engine.

We sat in front of his giant television watching vintage gay porn and smoking a joint. Once we finished smoking, he got to work. His throat seemed like an endless tunnel and he ate my asshole. I got worried when I felt some air escape.

He kept at it. He encouraged me to keep farting.

Each push seemed to bring me closer to a dump, but I was lost in the ecstasy of marijuana and a tongue loosening me up. I heard him moan and ask me to push.

I don't want to shit.

He smiled.

Just do it.

I shot up and ran to the bathroom. He stood at the threshold and watched me.

You could've done it in my mouth.

I wondered why the words excited me. Is this the sort of thing my stepmother warned me about? Was she right about these faggots leading me down a road of depravity? Was she right about me losing my soul in this world of dissolution? I walked to Queen to catch the 501 streetcar and the whole ride home, my erection refused to be contained. He had opened up a world from which I couldn't return.

The year 2016 was when I was worn, torn, and displaced. I moved a total of six times that year. I went from a roach-infested bachelor apartment in Parkdale to a room in a three-bedroom unit on Rosemount Avenue in Scarborough. I had enough of

Parkdale, and the rent was too high for what I was being paid for my job at a weight-loss clinic.

By now, my alcoholism had led me to lose my second job with a transit company. They fired me for falsifying records. What that actually meant was that I used to show up at 8 a.m. instead of my 6 a.m. start time. I didn't reflect this on my timesheet.

But I digress.

February 1, 2016, I moved into a Spanish woman's apartment in Scarborough. The reason she wanted me to move in was because my name was Islamic and she figured she had found a companion for her anti-Semitism. I had no interest in speculating whether the Zika virus was invented by Jews, or whether Spain was right for expelling their ancient Jewish community. She signified the collapse of what I called "white lies."

The year 2016 was when white lies that sustain this part of the world collapsed.

These lies originated in 1492 when Iberian voyagers set out to "discover" new lands. The ensuing five hundred years were a boon for European Christendom.

The decline was accelerated by the election of Trump by white Christians in the United States of America. One in two white women voted for Trump, yet white feminists never tired of reminding black women that gender superseded race. That's why 2016 is also when I ditched every single white woman in my life.

As summer came into full view that year, I moved to a vegan commune, close to Jean Sibelius Square Park, on Brunswick Avenue. The walls were covered with Free Palestine posters. The bathrooms were stocked with leftist literature, and maps showed the destruction the Canadian state imposed on the peoples of the First Nations. Anti-Semitism flowed as easily in the commune as it had with the Spanish woman in Scarborough. Why did people revert to their hatred of Jews? I didn't get it.

BRAVE OLD WORLD

My descent into homelessness actually began in the summer of 2015. I worked as a radio controller for the Pan American Games, one of the biggest sporting events in Toronto's history.

Three months in, I lost that gig because I failed to provide sufficient identification to receive a security clearance. Meanwhile, my domestic life wasn't faring any better. My landlady, the mother of my friend Venezia, told me an offer had been made for the house. I was happy for them since they had been trying to sell for several years.

The Polish people buying the house weren't keen on having a darkie living in their house. My landlady, eager to gloss over such obscenities, asked why I wanted to live there without her family? She offered to help me find a new apartment. Her real estate agent, a Palestinian woman, was helping an Albanian man and his father acquire a building on Maynard Avenue in Parkdale.

My landlady helped me with the first and last month's rent and with that solved the problem of evicting me. It was so effortless. It took a year to figure out how I got shafted. My rent, which had been $650, suddenly went up to $800, and I was making a third of what I used to make at my government job. But I wasn't going to cut them off until after I attended their daughter's wedding in the summer of 2016. I showed up with my hair in a bun and draped myself in an ultramarine silk shirt with matching pants.

I wore black-and-white oxfords. I didn't drink. Instead, I put weed tincture in my water and watched the groom's guests make fools of themselves. They flew in from France, and they were the worst. I felt joyous about severing all ties to these basic bitches.

★ ★ ★

As 2017 dawned, I got the chance to write this book, and Bruce, the lovely man at the University of Regina Press, believed in me and my story. I waited years for the chance to be published. The decline in my living standard persisted.

By June of 2017, I lived in a men's shelter at Lans-downe Avenue and Dupont Street. It was there that I met a young West Indian man who had dreadlocks and was named Tyrone. He didn't talk much, and after the shelter closed its Out of the Cold program, we parted ways.

The thing about homelessness was that it skewed everything that seemed normal and mundane about my life.

It meant rooms the size of an apartment filled with thirty or so bodies and, depending on where I stayed, pets. The bedbugs fed on our blood. I was among people with severe mental health issues, exacerbated by drug and alcohol abuse. Suspicion permeated the air, and all smiles were false. The street connections floundered despite proclamations of eternal friendship. The steam of their skin stirred me in my sleep. Their faces were gaunt and missing teeth. They spent their waking hours scamming each other. Every single one of them knew how to do the staff's jobs but couldn't find a job to save their lives. They didn't have the wherewithal to feed or clothe themselves. At breakfast, the men threatened each other and complained about the food.

No one is forcing you to be here.

The front desk handed out clean syringes, but I was not allowed to roll a joint at the table.

Meanwhile, Naloxone was deployed during lunch because a junkie shot up some unknown concoction.

Everyone go back to eating. He's fine.

The Sisters of the Order of Saint Felix came by to restock the crossword puzzles and counsel the degenerate souls in their care. They seemed so old and frail, yet their faith was stronger than anything I had to hold on to.

To the body of Christ we were called.

. . . But it was difficult to hear Him over lunatic ravings. Watch out for broken crack pipes on the piss-soaked floors of the bathroom.

★ ★ ★

As Canada celebrated its 150th birthday, I gazed out at Queen Street West from the bar I was in. I ordered my fifth margarita and watched a fellow vagrant sitting on the sidewalk, handcuffed.

I got drunk and my tooth abscessed. The filling had fallen out a while back, but I didn't tend to it. Oral health wasn't a major priority. I could've died, according to the dental surgeons at Mount Sinai who treated me.

As I walked up University Avenue, with gauze in my mouth, Canada Day revellers gawked at me.

Blood gushed onto the sidewalk as I passed the Ontario Power Building.

I slept under a tree behind Queen's Park that night as fireworks illuminated the Canadian skies.

By the grace of God, I woke up with no pain in my mouth.

Among Somalis in the West, there's a shame about our predicament.

As children of refugees we were told to do well. What did that entail? It meant going to school and getting good grades. Attending mosque and learning the ancient words of our ancient faith. It meant keeping away from the criminal element and avoiding infection by Western culture. Making sure we didn't forget how to speak our native tongue. If you were a Somali girl, wearing a hijab and dressing modestly were key.

Despite all these guidelines, many of us who grew up in the West found it difficult to do well, stay true to the faith, and continue speaking our language. The gap between imagined success and the lived experience was vast but pretending everything was fine was a wonderful byproduct of Somaliniimo.

Every time Ebyan ran away, my stepmother feigned ignorance about her absence or explained she was staying with friends out of town. This pattern repeated itself in every Somali community outside Somalia.

Little mention was made of that boy hauled off to jail. Everyone forgot so-and-so's sister who went mad and now lived on the streets. No one remembered that boy who joined the army of gays downtown.

A thick shame tied us together and it burned us up, but we paraded around as though everything was fine.

Eventually, a rift developed between the elders, who waxed nostalgically about a home they ruined and the youngsters. Grandparents found it difficult to converse with their grandchildren because they didn't speak Somali. Those brought from Somalia at the age of ten, eleven, or twelve found themselves alienated from our native culture and the one they had been adopted into.

The unacknowledged theme of our experience is the tendency for revision. Ask any Somali and they'll tell you that we've always been Muslims.

What was forgotten is that we used to worship a sky goddess named Waaq. Several places in Somalia were named after this deity. The unintended effect of revision is that it distorts our sense of ourselves.

Revisionism to cover up our history has been pervasive.

No one I know or am related to has any ties to the regime of Brother Siad. We are its victims.

None of us claim kinship with any of the warlords who ravaged the country.

But the only people who can claim no ties to the regime or the warlords are the Bantus. They are the descendants of freed slaves. Their lot has been one of misery and oppression at home, and in diaspora, they are overlooked and not considered one of us.

If we acknowledged them, we would have to be honest with ourselves.

The reality is that many of us had ties to the tawdry actors in our history. We all served Brother Siad. We all belonged to a clan whose militias ruined our ancestral home. Our ancestors were slave traders.

These are thorny issues, so revisionism serves as a cure-all for the suffering Somali.

One example of our shame was a man I met on the first day I was homeless for the second time.

I sat outside the men's shelter on Lansdowne having a smoke and locked eyes with a middle-aged Somali man. He wobbled over. He told me his name and asked for a cigarette. I asked if he sustained the injury back home. He let out a hearty laugh and said he wasn't a militiaman.

He joined a gang when his family arrived in Toronto in the early 1990s. They settled in the high-rises where I attended Quranic school. Since the schools in the area were predominantly West

Indian and white working class, the new arrivals found it difficult to get on. In order to protect each other from their schoolmates, they formed cliques of their own. Eventually, these cliques competed with the established gangs and the requisite tools of the trade entered the picture.

It was during the expansion of what was called the Dixon Bloods that my fellow vagrant was shot in the back. He stared off into the distance and told me he knew the guy who shot him.

If only I listened to my hoyo, I wouldn't be in this situation, wallahi.

A few days later, he was asked to leave the shelter because he sprayed a staff member with ketchup. The staff inquired if they could call anyone for him. We were in a room adjacent to the office and I overheard the shelter worker talking to his family. They claimed not to know him. It was shame that drove them to deny him.

FLAMES RAVAGING HIS
GLOWING HAIR

The drop-in centre I frequented during the day had a shelter upstairs and a bed was available. I was reunited with Tyrone. I sensed he was hiding something, but I didn't want to broach it with him. Young black men in the closet came with so many issues that it was next to impossible for me to open up any of it. His bed was beside mine and a barrier divided us.

Next to me, in the enclosed space, was a Central African man who identified as French. I rolled my eyes. He asked me about the city's intention to open safe injection sites. I told him about the opioid crisis and used the word *junkie* to describe opiate users. This is when Tyrone interrupted our conversation.

You are this close to being burned alive. You better watch how you talk. I'm a junkie.

I went downstairs and told the staff what transpired.

I want the police called.

I went for a walk to calm the fear washing over me. That night, back upstairs, I saw him sitting up in bed. I pretended to be asleep. As the staff changed shifts at midnight, he struck. He doused me in lighter fluid and chased me downstairs.

He's trying to kill me!

Tyrone passed by on his way out the door and calmly addressed the staff.

You guys ought to call the police!

The staff had no idea he was the culprit, so they ran upstairs, allowing him to escape. But the other residents ran after him and held him until police arrived. I collapsed on the floor of the dining hall and from the corner of my eye saw the others gawking at my shaking body. I looked at my arms and wondered how I was saved from being set on fire.

I gave my statement to the police and went for a walk. The streets were devoid of any traffic, and I burped up lighter fluid.

The next day I decided I was going to perform a pilgrimage, or *hajj* as Muslims called it. I had come so close to dying. No one in my past would've known of my death. I felt unmoored from reality and needed to remember that I existed at some point.

I set out to visit those places in Toronto that were critical to my current condition. I wanted to reclaim my past self as fuel for my future self. To blend my current thesis with its antithesis to synthesize a new Mohamed. By going on this journey, I wanted to liberate myself from the shackles of the past.

My first stop was gentrified Dundas Street West. I had spent many nights, and thousands of dollars, partying, being ejected, and sniffing cocaine there. I glided across the pavement and peeked into the bars where I had been a staple. I realized that this is where I attempted to become Canadian. I had worked a decent job, dressed in clothing from thrift shops, and spoke in the same lingo as the white hipsters I peopled my black life with. I came across one of them, and he acted like he didn't know me.

I ventured further east along Dundas. This was where I was exposed to the processes of gentrification, where I absorbed Fanon and de Sade.

I got off the subway and walked across Dundas Square. There was a concert going on, and in the background, the noise of construction was drowning out the music. I walked through the abandoned campus and beheld the new buildings.

Ryerson was seen by many in Toronto as a leftist alternative to the money-grubbing Anglo-centricity of the University of Toronto. I never understood that, because the people who ran Ryerson moved with ease to positions of power across the educational landscape. On the ground, the school displaced poor and homeless people from the east end.

Along Jarvis, Mutual, Church, Yonge, Dundas, Gerrard, and Carlton, I saw how the gleaming new buildings of Ryerson raised the rents and displaced communities to the inhospitable edges of metro Toronto. The downtown was a playground for yuppies who spent their youths in the suburbs.

Outside becomes inside, inside becomes outside.

My third stop was the Gordonridge neighbourhood. I got off at Midland Avenue and Danforth Road and noticed the old Price Chopper had been replaced by a Chinese grocery store. Many of the other businesses were still there. I lit a smoke and crossed the plaza to the pink and blue buildings where I had spent three years crying, laughing, being hungover, having sex, and hosting friends. The balconies were being replaced. I passed an older West Indian woman who wished me a blessed day. God bless black women.

My fourth landing place was the site of my suicide attempt. I took the 89 Weston bus from Keele station, and the Somalis aboard the bus glared at me. I looked more femme than usual, and my clutch, from the dollar store, was red and see-through. I kept my head high, unwilling to let their intrusive glances discourage me. I got off at Denison Road and walked the final kilometre up to Lawrence.

I saw the gleaming building for the first time in twelve years. I hadn't bothered to venture up to the town of Weston in the years that I'd lived on my own. I didn't understand that by revisiting the past I could make peace with the future. As I walked down Hickory Tree Road, something was trying to escape my body.

As I walked around the entirety of the building, the tears welled up.

I perused the commercial strip of Weston and saw my younger self, unsure of his step, moving ahead of me. I was a fierce queen now, and I wasn't going to make any apologies for it. On my way to the library on King Street, I passed a Somali vagrant. I gave him my last joint and two cigarettes. He wanted to kiss my hand and I let him.

My final destination was my old school, C.W. Jefferys.

I walked into the grocery store at Jane Finch Mall and behind me was a young man with a cognac bottle. He offered me a swig and I offered him a toonie. He threw it on the ground, and I shrugged.

Bun you!

No kind act goes unpunished.

I made my way along Finch, and as I got closer to the school, my heart raced. Over the summer in 2017, a student drowned while on a school trip to a provincial park. According to his parents, his teachers assured them that their son knew how to swim.

The year 2017 also marked the tenth anniversary of Jordan Manners's death. A student at C.W. Jefferys, Jordan had been shot by his classmate. The event marked the first time a student had been shot inside a Toronto school.

I sat beneath the flagpole and cried.

I cried for all the souls that didn't see their lives continue past their stay at Jefferys.

The people across the street were mowing their lawns. The suburban quietness of Sentinel Road was at odds with the eruption of feeling.

Auden once wrote that suffering can take place *while someone else is eating or opening a window or just walking dully along.*

As I returned to the shelter, I reached out to one of the shelter workers. She took me outside so we could have more privacy. She asked what I was up to.

I went to go find myself.

I broke down, and she held me. I smelled the cocoa butter through her shirt.

I think I am an alcoholic. I need help.

You're very brave. Dry your tears and go for a walk. When you come back, I'll give you some numbers. Remember, you're worth it.

SELECTED BIBLIOGRAPHY

Andrzejewski, B.W., and Sheila Andrzejewski, trans. *An Anthology of Somali Poetry*. Bloomington: Indiana University Press, 1993.

Auden, W.H. *Selected Poems by W.H. Auden*. Compiled by Edward Mendelson. New York City, NY: Vintage Books, 1979.

Ballard, J.G. *The Atrocity Exhibition*. London: Fourth Estate, 2014.

———. *Concrete Island*. New York: Picador/Farrar, Straus & Giroux, 2018.

———. *Crash*. Los Angeles: Rare Bird Books, 2019.

Courtenay, Bryce. *The Power of One*. Penguin Group Australia, 1998.

Cuning, William Waring. "No Images" from *Storefront Church*. Paul Breman Limited, 1973.

De Heilige Ayaan (The Holy Ayaan). Directed by Jos Van Dongen. Netherlands: BNNVARA, 2006. Televised Documentary.

Fanon, Frantz. *Toward the African Revolution: Political Essays*. New York: Grove Press, 2004.

Haar, Jaap Ter. *Boris*. Translated by Martha Mearns and illustrated by Rien Poortvliet. Neerlandia, AB, Canada: Inheritance Publications, 2009.

Hughes, Langston. *The Big Sea*. New York & London: Knopf, 1940.

Jefferys, C.W. *Canada's Past in Pictures*. Toronto, ON: Ryerson, 1934.

Ovid. *Metamorphoses*. Translated by A.D. Melville. Oxford, UK: Oxford University Press, 2009.

Sade, Marquis de. *The Marquis de Sade: The 120 Days of Sodom, and Other Writings*. Compiled and translated by Austryn Wainhouse and Richard Seaver. New York: Grove Press, 1978.

The Trap: What Happened to Our Dream of Freedom. Directed by Adam Curtis. United Kingdom: BBC, 2007. Televised Documentary.

Wright, Richard. *Black Boy (American Hunger): A Record of Childhood and Youth*. New York: Harper Perennial Modern Classics, 2008.

——. *Native Son*. Philadelphia: Chelsea House Publishers, 1988.

ABOUT THE AUTHOR

Mohamed Abdulkarim Ali was born in Mogadishu, Somalia, and lived in the United Arab Emirates and the Netherlands before immigrating to Canada as a teenager. He currently lives in Toronto. This is his first book.

A NOTE ON THE TYPE

This book is set in *Athelas*, a serif typeface designed by Veronika Burian and Jose Scaglione and intended for use in body text. Released by the company Type-Together in 2008, Burian and Scaglione described *Athelas* as inspired by British fine book printing.

The accents are set in *Phosphate*, an all-caps sans serif font family with an inline weight, created by Steve Jackaman (ITF) and Ashley Muir in 2010. The original *Phosphate* was published by International TypeFounders, and the family was based on the 'Phosphor' typeface created by Jakob Erbar for Ludwig and Mayer, circa 1922–30.

Text and cover design by Duncan Noel Campbell, University of Regina Press.

THE REGINA COLLECTION

Named as a tribute to Saskatchewan's capital city with its rich history of boundary-defying innovation, *The Regina Collection* builds upon University of Regina Press's motto of "a voice for many peoples." Intimate in size and beautifully packaged, these books aim to tell the stories of those who have been caught up in social and political circumstances beyond their control.

To see other books in *The Regina Collection,* visit
www.uofrpress.ca